The Primary Teacher's Guide to

Writing

• Key subject knowledge • Background information • Teaching tips •

D1136497

❚❚SCHOLASTIC

Book End, Range Road, Witney, Oxfordshire, OX29 0YD
www.scholastic.co.uk
© 2013 Scholastic Ltd
1 2 3 4 5 6 7 8 9   3 4 5 6 7 8 9 0 1 2

British Library Cataloguing-in-Publication Data
A catalogue record for this book is available from the British Library.

ISBN 978-1407-12795-8
Printed and bound by CPI Group (UK) Ltd, Croydon, CR0 4YY

Author
Eileen Jones

Editorial team
Rachel Morgan, Melissa Rugless, Niamh O'Carroll, Marion Archer

Indexer
Jane Read

Series Designers
Shelley Best and Sarah Garbett

Typesetter
Ricky Capanni (International Book Management)

Icons
Tomek.gr

Acknowledgements
The publishers gratefully acknowledge permission to reproduce the following copyright material:

John Foster for the use of 'Count Dracula' from *The Works: Poems* edited by Paul Cookson. Poem © 2000, John Foster (2000, Macmillan). **Sue Cowling** for the use of 'Penguin' from *The Works: Poems* edited by Paul Cookson. Poem © 2000, Sue Cowling (2000, Macmillan). **David Higham Associates** for the use of 'Undersea Tea' from *The Works: Poems* edited by Paul Cookson. Poem © 2000, Tony Mitton (2000, Macmillan). **Nick Toczek** for the use of 'The Dragon Ate Our School' from *Dragons!* by Nick Toczek. Poem © 2005, Nick Toczek (2005, Macmillan). **Penguin Books Ltd** for the use of 'Please Mrs Butler' from *Please Mrs Butler: Verses* by Allan Ahlberg. Poem © 1983, Allan Ahlberg (1983, Kestrel Books). **Coral Rumble** for the use of 'Cats Can' from *The Works: Poems* edited by Paul Cookson. Poem © 2000, Coral Rumble (2000, Macmillan). **Roger Stevens** for the use of 'Louder!' from *Custard Pie* edited by Pie Corbett. Poem © 1996, Roger Stevens (1996, Macmillan). **Anthony Thwaite** for the use of 'The Fly' from *Collected Poems* by Anthony Thwaite. Poem © 2007, Anthony Thwaite (2007, Enitharmon Press). **Jill Townsend** for the use of 'When Leaves Pile Up' from *The Works: Poems* edited by Paul Cookson. Poem © 2000, Jill Townsend (2000, Macmillan). **Colin West** for the use of 'Toboggan' and 'Socks' from *The Best of West* by Colin West. Poem © 1990, Colin West (1990, Hutchinson). **Bernard Young** for the use of 'Career Opportunity: Knight Required' from *Brilliant* by Bernard Young. Poem © 2000, Bernard Young (2000, Kingston Press).

Every effort has been made to trace copyright holders for the works reproduced in this book, and the publishers apologise for any inadvertent omissions.

Contents

Icon key

Information within this book is highlighted in the margins by a series of different icons. They are:

Subject facts
Key subject knowledge is clearly presented and explained in this section.

Why you need to know these facts
Provides justification for understanding the facts that have been explained in the previous section.

Vocabulary
A list of key words, terms and language relevant to the preceding section. Vocabulary entries appear in the glossary.

Amazing facts
Interesting snippets of background knowledge to share.

Common misconceptions
Identifies and corrects some of the common misconceptions and beliefs that may be held about the subject area.

Teaching ideas
Outlines practical teaching suggestions using the knowledge explained in the preceding section.

Questions
Identifies common questions and provides advice on how to answer them.

Handy tips
Specific tips or guidance on best practice in the classroom.

Writing

I don't
Know what
to write.
My
Classmates
Seem much
Slicker.
If I
write like
this,
I'll fill
my page
much
quicker!
                by Tracey Blance

Does this poem reflect the attitude of your class? Yet writing should be enjoyable for children! After all, it starts as a basic urge. Babies and toddlers – long before nursery and primary schools take up their formal education – delight in 'making their mark' with whatever implement comes to hand. However, this uninhibited ability to be writers can waver. Children going through primary school recognise that writing means more than making random marks, and become self-critical. As they compare their results with texts they read, they want to acquire some of the skills they see there.

What do teachers need to know?

● **The correct words:** Teachers need the vocabulary of writing. Children will ask for the names of genres, literary devices, types of words, unusual writing forms, sections of writing, special features and organisational devices.

● **Distinctions and connections:** People use words carelessly. Teachers must be ready to explain differences between often-confused terms: 'similes' and 'metaphors'; 'alliteration' and 'assonance'; 'biographies' and 'autobiographies'; 'articles' and 'reports'; 'myths' and 'legends'. They must be ready to explain that fiction can be linked to real life, with stories about issues or other cultures; that the speech written for a character should connect with the actions described; and that a moral may be contained in more than one type of story.

● **Up-to-date information:** There are new forms of writing. Electronic writing has brought new vocabulary and new conventions. Terms such as 'email', 'document', 'attachment' and 'subject line' may be optional in adults' writing experience; for the children, they will become essential knowledge. The technical terminology of 'ebooks', 'online newspapers' and 'message boards' needs to be kept up with and understood. These different forms and their impact on writing must become part of the teacher's factfile.

● **Where examples of writing can be found:** You need to know where different forms of writing can be seen. You must be able to recognise a chronological report, a newspaper article, a kenning or a myth. Practical teaching necessitates showing children exemplars of different writing forms.

● **How to move from theory into practice:** Facts are little use on their own! There is a need to be able to translate the theory of these facts into the practice of writing. How much emphasis should be put on planning? What is an effective way to construct a story structure? What is a suitable title when writing an explanation? These are the details that enable the teacher to help children progress from knowing to writing.

The aims of this book
● **Fill the knowledge gaps:** The knowledge required by teachers of writing is summarised above. This book aims to provide that knowledge, as well as filling in the other information relevant to each genre of writing.

- **Offer support:** Reading is one thing; remembering is quite another. This book aims to be the teacher's backup, there to refer to and check in whenever needed. Most primary teachers are not literacy specialists and this book's aim is to be supportive, whatever the teacher's initial level of writing confidence or competence.

- **Provide inspiration:** Patchy answers or dry information will not necessarily produce the pieces of writing you had hoped for. Children must feel inspired to write – the tasks and the writing activities that you suggest must motivate them. Of course, you have your own fund of ideas, but every teacher is grateful for a fresh supply. This book aims to replenish those ideas.

- **Answer questions:** The book aims to anticipate additional questions and to answer them, without overloading the teacher with information.

How the book is organised
This book is divided into six chapters, which in turn are divided into sections:

- **Chapter 1 Planning fiction:** This chapter covers the basic features that can be found in all stories and explores ways to plan stories.

- **Chapter 2 Writing fiction:** The chapter divides fiction writing into five story types and provides a section of information, advice and teaching ideas on each: traditional stories; adventure and mystery; imagined worlds; real issues; writing about other times and cultures.

- **Chapter 3 Non-fiction:** A section is allocated to writing each of these eight text types: reports; recounts; explanations; instructions; discussion texts; persuasion texts; biographies and autobiographies; texts that add information. There is also a section on planning and preparation for writing an effective non-fiction text.

- **Chapter 4 Poetry:** This chapter has nine sections. Three sections cover fundamental tools of poetry:

rhyme; rhythm and sound; imagery. Further sections cover a wide range of poetry forms including: humour and nonsense verse; narrative poems; performance poems; poems with a structure; shape poetry. The initial section provides what you need to consider before writing poetry.

● **Chapter 5 Playscripts:** Playscript writing is divided into six areas: planning; dialogue; presenting characters; plays for stage and screen; plays for listening; story adaptation. Each area provides examples of the writing style covered.

● **Chapter 6 Media:** The chapter provides six sections which look at different aspects of media writing: reports and articles; editorials; advertisements; correspondence to the media; the alternative presentation of newspapers and magazines. There is an additional introductory section on planning and preparing to write media texts.

Getting the most from this book

● **Dip in and out:** Keep returning to the book as and when you need it. You may only spend one week on playwriting early in the year but you will probably return to it later. Use the book in the same way, not as something to read from start to finish but to be read in the order that suits what you are doing.

● **Check your plan:** Make the book fit in with your planned Scheme of Work. Check when, for example, your first poetry work is scheduled and take time to read and absorb the first section of this book's poetry chapter beforehand. Then read the section relating to the poetry you plan to study and write.

● **Use the glossary:** You might come across unfamiliar terms in this book. That's what the book's glossary is there for: to act as a writing dictionary, support your explanations to the children and give you confidence.

● **Consider the resources:** Each chapter finishes with a list of the resources used or recommended for that chapter. If you find that one area of writing is presenting particular difficulties, a publication from this reading list may help.

● **Use the teaching ideas:** Every section of every chapter has a list of teaching ideas. Some can be interlinked, offering opportunities for extended writing by building on one another, while others offer useful activities that can be incorporated into your lesson plans.

● **Be adventurous:** There are inspiring teaching ideas to support the teacher in this book, but they also lend themselves to adaptation, extension or substitution. Make a change to the game suggested, substitute different writing features, change the type of poem or add a character. In this way, the teaching idea will be refreshed and the children newly inspired.

In conclusion...

This is a book to support the primary teacher. It aims to pass on subject knowledge and to provide the means to teach concepts and skills more confidently. It does not require the reader to be a literacy specialist. The text is not overly academic and the presentation aims to be user-friendly. The beginning of this introduction mentions children being self-critical and ambitious to produce writing more like the texts they read. Through this book, they will feel that they have been shown the way.

True ease in writing comes from art, not chance,
As those who move easiest who have learned to dance.

From *An Essay on Criticism* by Alexander Pope

Chapter 1

Planning fiction

Planning is the key to successful story writing. It brings order and discipline to the imaginative ideas of fiction. There is no right or wrong in story planning; after all, it will be a guide for that writer. Nevertheless, the finished story will have certain writing elements and a conventional order. So the children should consider these in their plan.

Planning a story

Subject facts

The main building blocks of any story are the characters, setting and plot.

Character

The characters are the people (or sometimes animals or other creatures) in the story. A plan may not identify every character to be written about, but main characters and some characteristics should be noted, perhaps in a one-word note about personality, family background or job/school. Plans could include a sketch showing an unexpected action or how and when new characteristics are going to be revealed.

Setting

The setting is the place and time in which the story's events occur. The place could be real (such as London), imaginary (such as Neverland), specific (such as Charing Cross Road, London) or general (such as a kitchen). The time could be present day, historic, the future or 'timeless' – as in fairy tales, for example. A specific date could be mentioned, or details such as clothing, technology and speech may put a story into a specific time period. When planning a story children should consider how this may be represented. Also, the setting may change during the story, either through a movement in time or a change in location.

Plot

The plot is the action of the story. These are the events that form the story's framework, so this chronological timeline is essential to the plan. The plot may have several layers and developments; this is looked at in more detail in the next section.

It is important to also mention that the genre, or type, of story that is planned can influence plot, character and setting. Chapter 2 looks at different genres in more detail.

Why you need to know these facts

● The children ought to have the vocabulary of fiction: 'setting', 'character' and 'plot' are fundamental to narrative writing. Understanding the words will inform the children of the questions to ask of their plan: *Who? What? Where? How?* The correct vocabulary will also give them the confidence to speak with authority about their intended writing.

● By planning plot, characters and setting you can help children to avoid the common mistake of including many unnecessary characters which distract from the plot or too many settings.

Vocabulary

Character – a person (or creature) in a fictional piece of writing.
Genre – a grouping of similar texts.
Plot – the timeline of events in a story.
Setting – the place, time or environment in which events occur.

Teaching ideas

These activities will often result in a story plan. Keep these plans for use in the Teaching ideas of later chapters.

● Explore stories that the children are familiar with and ask them to identify the characters (and characteristics), setting (location and time) and plot within them. This will aid the children in using these effectively in their own writing.

● Ask the children to create a writing frame on which an author could plan a story opening. Provide three headings: *Setting*, *Character*, *Plot*. For each, can they write a single-word question which, when answered, will provide relevant information? (For example, *Where? Who? What?*) Can they add further short questions, allowing space for the answers in written notes? A second, improved version of the writing frame may be necessary.

● Use a novel's opening chapters, or a short story, for the children to test their planning frames by answering their questions, in notes. Afterwards discuss findings. Was there enough space? Did the questions produce relevant answers?

● Hold discussions about a main character in a story already read. Let the children take the author's place when making planning notes under this title question: *What will my character be like*? Suggest a planning format: the character's name or picture in the centre, surrounded by six empty circles. Each circle could have a heading: *Appearance*; *Attitude to possessions*; *Speech*; *Honesty*; *Attitude to others*; *Self-confidence*. Can the children, pretending to be the author, write notes in each circle, saying what, how and when they will reveal to the reader about this characteristic?

Focusing on plot

Subject facts

As discussed in the last section, the plot is the action of a story. For younger children, this will often be broken down to:

- Beginning – how does the story start?
- Middle – what happens? (A problem or event.)
- End – how is it resolved?

For older children, this should be developed into a story sequence such as presented below. The story sequence is the path that the main plot follows. There is an expected order of events in the story, and hence in the plan:

- **Opening:** In the opening, the story's setting is established and some main characters are introduced.
- **Problem:** This is the climax of the story, when something happens that is a problem or puzzle.
- **Resolution:** The resolution comprises the events that sort out and supply an answer to the problem.
- **Ending:** The ending brings the main plot and any subplots (see below) to a conclusion. All questions posed in the story should now be answered, and the writer may form a link with the beginning of the story.

Subplots

Subplots are minor plots that run in parallel with the main plot. As the children's story writing becomes more ambitious, subplots will allow them to keep the stories interesting. More intricate plans must allow for them. The subplots must link to the main plot – through character or place – and, at some point in the story, meet.

Why you need to know these facts

● Fiction is made up and so it is easy for writers to become overwhelmed by their ideas as their imagination leads them down different paths. Planning forces the writer to focus and to produce the basic framework of the story's structure. The writer can dispense with ideas that are not relevant to the story, yet still add new detail when writing. With a plan, it will be clear if and where those new ideas fit in.

● Planning is part of the process of writing fiction and understanding this will help the children to progress as writers. They will realise that the authors whom they admire and read also plan. Telling them that JK Rowling had planned her whole series of *Harry Potter* books before writing the first one, and that planning is one of Michael Morpurgo's tips for story-writing success, will emphasise this message.

Vocabulary

Subplot – a minor plot that runs in parallel with the main plot.

Teaching ideas

● Encourage children to look at books they are familiar with to see how the opening, problem, resolution and ending are structured and to make notes about them. Are there any similarities between things that they read?

● When looking at subplots, ask the children to plan the main backbone of the story first, before looking at how to extend it. This will help to avoid any unnecessary tangents and a never-ending plot line. You could: provide the main structure of a story for them to add subplots to; identify the character, place or object that will form the link; provide cards of subplots for the children to choose appropriate ones to add into their stories.

Chapters

A chapter is a section of the story. It is a useful way for the writer to organise the text and to allow the reader a break in concentration. It is also a helpful place for the writer to change the focus of character, setting or plot. Chapters become important as the children write longer, more complex stories. In *The Railway Children*, E Nesbit uses a new chapter as an opportunity to provide more detail about a main character, as this opening paragraph from chapter 7 demonstrates:

> *I hope you don't mind my telling you a good deal about Roberta. The fact is I am growing very fond of her. The more I observe her the more I love her. And I notice all sorts of things about her that I like.*

Cliffhanger

A cliffhanger is a break in the story at a time when the future is unclear: an important character may have a problem, be in danger or face a dilemma. The audience is left wondering what is going to happen.

Cliffhanger moments may end chapters, particularly at the climax of the plot. They are an effective writing device for holding reader interest and urging the reader on. For example, at the end of a chapter halfway through *Charlotte's Web*, EB White leaves the reader puzzled about what Charlotte can be weaving into the open space in her web.

● Considering how you might break up a story into sections, or 'chapters', helps you focus on the organisation of the story.

- It can also help you focus on key areas of the plot to create tension through the use of cliffhangers, to make your reader want to continue reading.

Vocabulary

Chapter – a section of writing extending over a number of pages. A change of chapter often heralds the writer's change of focus to a different character or event.

Cliffhanger – a writing device in which a break occurs in the story when an important character is in danger, or faces a dilemma. The reader is left wondering what will happen.

Amazing facts

The term 'cliffhanger' is thought to have come from the silent adventure films of about 1900, in which a character was left in great danger at the end of an episode, sometimes actually hanging from the edge of a cliff. The audience had to wait for the next episode to see if the character would be saved.

Teaching ideas

- Have a discussion about cliffhangers – encourage the children to talk about TV shows or books where cliffhangers keep them on the edge of their seats. Liken the end of an episode, or the middle before an advert break, to the end of a book's chapter. What similarities and differences are there?

- Write down the main events of a story on small cards and jumble them up (including more than one event per chapter works well). In groups, ask the children to arrange the cards in plot order and discuss the best opportunities for chapter breaks in the story.

Planning frames

Subject facts

Story planning may take any form. It is usually in notes and phrases, not sentences, and organisational devices such as boxes and shapes are often used. Plot chronology may be indicated by numbers or arrows. Although there is no set format, these are useful examples that can be modelled for the children or given as prepared frames to be filled in.

Storyboard

A storyboard consists of a sequence of pictures that show the plot of a story in the order in which events will happen. The plan is made by the writer and is a reminder of where the story is leading. Even very early writers will cope well with this form of planning, especially when they are given a starting point and encouraged to act out or talk about what their characters may do.

As children get older, they may be encouraged to include more detail in the pictures or have brief accompanying text. When writing the story, these will jog their memories and help the writing process for a more detailed story.

● **Numbers and labels:** A page divided into four numbered, headed squares is an effective storyboard for young writers. Children would be required to draw pictures under the headings:
1. Opening
2. Something happens
3. Events to sort it out
4. Ending

The children can progress to these labels:
1. Opening
2. Problem
3. Resolution
4. Ending

● **Prompts and questions:** For older writers, an extra box in the storyboard may be useful (or labels, prompts and questions as appropriate to a story theme). For example, for a story with a traditional hero and villain:

Opening	Build-up	Climax
Introduction of 'good' and 'bad' characters. What is their shared interest?	What happens? What do the good and bad characters do?	What is the good character in danger of? What problem is there?
Resolution How is the problem fixed?	**Ending** How does the story end? Will the characters keep their shared interest?	

Story mountain

The planning frame of a story mountain emphasises that a story builds up in detail and complexity. As the 'mountain' is ascended, so the writer adds to the plot. The climax will come at the peak. The plan can allow for a more complex story by extending the mountain into a range.

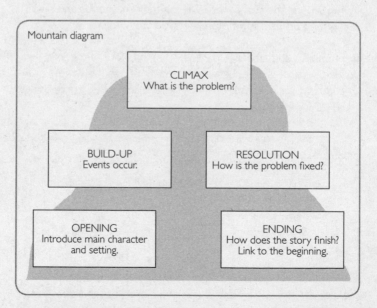

Mountain diagram

CLIMAX
What is the problem?

BUILD-UP
Events occur.

RESOLUTION
How is the problem fixed?

OPENING
Introduce main character and setting.

ENDING
How does the story finish? Link to the beginning.

Structure map

As writers increase the complexity of their stories, their effective plans also grow more complex. Narrative structure maps emphasise that story events, problems and answers are likely to be numerous. The final resolution may indeed be part of the story's ending. The children should be encouraged to adapt a map to their own needs and perhaps use a large piece of paper.

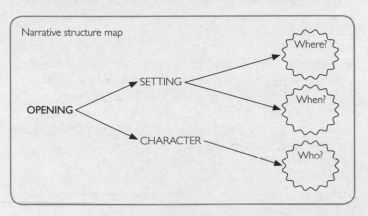

Narrative structure map

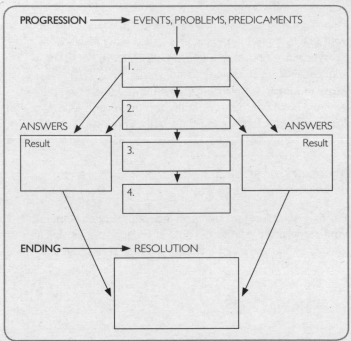

Why you need to know these facts

● Wanting to plan is one thing, knowing how to is another. Storyboards, story mountains and structure maps all provide effective examples. From these, the children may select what is appropriate to their current writing needs. Amending and improving to find a planning style to suit their proposed story will be a natural progression.

● Narrative structure maps can grow in complexity to match writing ability and ambitions. Children can use a large piece of paper, or a computer's symbols, shapes and easy movement of text. The plan could be multi-layered with a hyperlink to a subplot or character detail. As writers, the children will appreciate the benefits of thorough planning.

Vocabulary

Planning frame – a page of linked headings, boxes and shapes with spaces for notes and pictures to aid story planning.
Storyboard – a planning frame, usually pictorial, consisting of sequential boxes to match the story's plot.
Story mountain – a planning frame in the shape of a mountain, with the climax of the story at the top, and events leading to and from the climax forming the sides of the mountain.

Common misconceptions

Planning is not just for novices. In fact, experienced authors of long, complicated stories rely on it in order that their writing weaves all the threads of their storylines or series together.

Handy tip

Remember that your plan is only a guide to what you think you will write. Additions, alterations and deletions can be made as your writing and thoughts progress.

Teaching ideas

These activities will often result in a story plan. Keep these plans for use in the Teaching ideas of later chapters.

● Ask the children to create a simple, complete storyboard for early writers, such as a Year 2 class. They could write their own version of a familiar tale from, for example, 'Cinderella' or 'Hansel and Gretel'. Let groups present and explain their storyboards to one another or the class.

● Agree on a common theme for a story. For example: fantasy; science fiction; imagined worlds (see also, Chapter 2). Share ideas before completing individual copies of 'Narrative structure map' on page 19 with written notes. Share results in groups. Make computers available with a template of the 'Narrative structure map' for the children to copy their plan into. Do they need to alter the plan? Will they delete or enlarge boxes, move a word, add a shape? Save the computer work for the next activity.

● Talk through the proposed, straightforward story of an exemplar, completed electronic plan from the previous task. Suggest adding at least one subplot. Demonstrate using a separate document for a simple plan – three vertical boxes linked by arrows. How could this be added to the main plan? Could one word form a hyperlink? Let the children return to their saved narrative structure map to add subplots, each as a separate document, and insert hyperlinks.

Planning fiction

Resources

How to Teach Story Writing at KS1 by Pie Corbett (Letts)
How to Teach Fiction Writing at KS2 by Pie Corbett (Letts)
How to Teach Writing Across the Curriculum by Sue Palmer
 (Routledge Publishers)
Write out of the Classroom: How to use the outdoors to inspire and create amazing writing by Colin Macfarlane
 (Routledge Publishers)

Writing fiction

Fiction is the 'Land of Make Believe', and it is open to everybody. Listen to toddlers at play, as they talk to themselves, their teddy or one another: they slip naturally from reality into fiction. This is what writers let themselves do. Once you remind the children that story making and storytelling come easily after years of practice, they will believe in themselves as writers. The stumbling block of the blank page will have gone. Planning fiction (see Chapter 1) and knowing the key features of the different genres will help children to write effectively and focus their writing.

Writing traditional stories

Subject facts

Traditional stories have oral roots. Their plots, therefore, are usually easy to remember, their characters sometimes stereotypical and their endings may be predictable. The stories often contain harsh events and the writer normally has a lesson to impart to the reader. The writer has no voice in the story, and so writes in the third person, using third-person pronouns: *he*; *she*; *it*; *her*; *him*; *they*; *them*.

There are a number of different categories of story that may be described as traditional.

Fairy tales

The fairy-tale genre is one that children will be familiar with and these stories all have similar features. Whether adapting known fairy tales or creating new ones, the following aspects should be considered.

- **Background:** Fairy tales come from a long history of stories that have evolved within the folklore of many cultures across the world. In the early 19th century the Brothers Grimm published collections of fairy tales from across Europe, which popularised stories such as 'Snow White' and 'Cinderella' and encouraged the success of other fairy-tale writers including Hans Christian Andersen.

- **Characters:** Recognisable characters are important. A clear demarcation between 'good' (virtuous) and 'bad' (villainous) characters is needed. Fairy tales take in a wide range of characters, often including kings, queens, princes, princesses, poor or rich, wise or foolish characters and sometimes magical characters such as elves, pixies and goblins. Appearance can also be made relevant, for example, the good Cinderella is kind and pretty and the bad Stepsisters are ugly. The writer needs to support these character stereotypes with appropriate actions and dialogue.

- **Plot:** The plot will often involve the hero/heroine searching for something (love, a home, wisdom) and many will involve magic to help them find it. There are many typical themes that can be explored: good and evil; rich and poor; wise and foolish; beautiful and ugly, and so on. Usually the story will be written in chronological order.

- **Setting:** The setting is usually vague, often written as though it was set in the past but without a specific historic setting. It is usually generic and can often follow similar traits to the characters – the villainous character will often live somewhere dark and spooky and the good character somewhere dilapidated with a change in setting by the end to somewhere much better.

- **Language:** Traditional opening words are *Once upon a time…*, but there are other variations such as: *A long, long time ago…*; *Once there lived…*; *There was once…* The aim is to advise the reader of the type of story coming and set it vaguely in the past. The closing words are often *They all lived happily ever after.* These words provide the happy, safe ending typical of a fairy tale. Children may also want to consider employing repetition to reinforce a message and to make it memorable. In 'The Three Little Pigs', the writer can emphasise the wolf's actions and the danger of quick, lazy work with *the wolf huffed and he puffed and he blew the house down.* Dialogue is also often a feature of fairy tales.

- **Message:** Often the simple story will convey a lesson about how people should behave. The children will need to consider this when planning and writing their story. For example: Red Riding Hood realises the foolishness of dawdling in the woods; Hansel and Gretel's father understands the folly of listening to cruel plans. The writer must let good characters be rewarded for their kind deeds, yet there may be forgiveness for villains – Cinderella marries a prince, but she may invite her wicked Stepsisters to come to the palace.

Fable

A fable is a short story that is written to convey a useful moral lesson. There are distinctive features that should be considered when writing.

- **Background:** Fables have different roots. Some have oriental traditions, but the most well known have been handed down from the Greek and Roman cultures. Fables further developed in the Middle Ages in France, and in later centuries in Italy, Spain and Germany. The 18th century was the golden age of the fable when its concepts about man and society drew the interest of philosophers.

- **Characters:** The main characters are usually animals and there are often only two of them. The writer should treat them as people and begin their names with capital letters – for example, *the Tortoise raced the Hare.* It is important to note that there is not much character development in these stories; the purpose of them is to provide a lesson.

- **Plot:** The plot must form a complete story. It is the most important part of a fable. The writer should keep the story short and easy to understand, but make the events clever or amusing. There is an understanding between the storyteller and reader that a fable is fictitious and that the events did not really take place – they form a narrative metaphor.

- **Setting:** The setting is usually inconsequential and generic without much description.

- **Language:** The writer should use a straightforward tone in the story, so that the reader will readily understand the plot. Human verbs and descriptions can be used about the animals. For example: *The **boastful** Hare **gloated** when the Tortoise **agreed** to a race.* Connectives are frequent within the text including temporal connectives (one morning, first, then). Simple dialogue may also be included.

- **Message:** The writer needs to write a lesson called a 'moral' after the main story, and place it underneath the main text. The children must ensure the moral's wording conveys a clear message to the reader, has an obvious link with the story and makes no mention of animals. They may find it useful to have a particular moral in mind before planning the rest of the story. The moral for 'The Hare and the Tortoise' is *Never give up as perseverance can win the day.*

A parable is similar to a fable, except the story usually contains a spiritual or religious moral.

Myth
Myths were often developed to explain the world, show cultural or spiritual beliefs, or convey traditions.

- **Background:** Myths have varied roots: some have arisen as over-elaborated accounts of historical events; some have explained a ritual; some make sense of natural phenomena. Early Greek myths evolved across Europe during the Renaissance Age.

- **Characters:** Similar characters to other traditional tales appear here – they can include heroes/heroines, talking animals, supernatural creatures, gods, kings and so on. There is usually a character who is the opposite of the hero (good and evil, weak and strong, and so on). Characterisation is important as they are often larger-than-life characters.

- **Plot:** The story often contains a journey, quest or a series of trials for the hero or heroine to undertake.

- **Setting:** Myths are usually set in the past during an unspecified time period. The setting tends to be dramatic and enhances the action – a dark forest, a labyrinth and so on.

- **Language:** The writer should use powerful imagery in descriptions of the appearance and sounds of horrible monsters, and in the powerful actions and revenge of heroic gods. There is more description and often less dialogue than some of the other types of traditional tale.

- **Message:** The writer often uses a myth to explain a fact in nature or a mysterious phenomenon. For example, writing a story about an angry god throwing bolts of thunder down to punish disobedient humans on earth could explain thunderstorms. A myth may also be written to emphasise a character's heroic exploits.

Legend

Myths and legends are similar. Usually a legend is portrayed as something that actually happened or could plausibly have happened in history (such as Robin Hood) although many have been considerably embellished.

- **Background:** Legends stem from all around the world, including Egyptian, Greek, Roman, English, Celtic, Indian, Chinese and Norse cultures. The stories are traditional historical tales popularly regarded as true, but usually containing a mixture of fact and fiction. There are often numerous versions of the same legend, such as those about Robin Hood, with the facts and the character of the hero becoming exaggerated over time. Legends about Robin Hood were told, and later written down, as far back as the 1300s.

- **Characters:** The writer's main characters are human heroes, such as King Arthur. Often a legend is focused on a single main character, although sometimes the focus could be the setting (Atlantis), an object (the holy grail) or an animal (the Loch Ness Monster).

- **Plot:** The plot may be based on truth, but the writer will usually embellish this original truth with new fictional details and ideas. Certainly, the writer must describe acts of bravery and daring deeds, and may include battles and fights. A legend is usually written in chronological order, and can often cover the whole life of a character in different episodes (such as the legend of King Arthur). If they are basing a story on a character's life, then breaking the story down into different episodes and focusing on one will provide children with a better focus for writing.

● **Setting:** Sometimes legends will be set during an unspecified time and in other stories there will be historic details that place them, such as in Robin Hood and the Crusades. The settings vary depending on the origin of the legend and the storyline but often contain descriptions.

● **Language:** Imagery is a feature of these stories. Words such as *noble, honourable* and *brave* are appropriate choices for the writer when describing a hero in a legend. Always the writer must aim to emphasise the hero's courage, so there is a need for powerful images for the reader. Symbolic language may also be used – red to indicate danger, darkness for evil and so on.

● **Message:** The writer must distinguish between honour and dishonour in the characters and their actions. The finished piece of writing should prove that honourable actions bring success and that good defeats evil.

Why you need to know these facts

● Traditional stories are the roots of story writing. They began as oral forms and hence often changed as they were retold. Knowing that these stories have evolved will afford children the writing freedom to elaborate on details in their own versions, make plot changes and assign different characteristics, while reproducing the recognisable tale.

● The story labels are important pieces of information for a writer of traditional stories. Words such as 'legend', 'myth', 'fable', 'parable' and 'fairy tale' are often used carelessly and incorrectly. Knowing the features, and the similarities and differences between them, will give the children understanding of what they are writing and the confidence to try a form that is new to them.

● Traditional stories are part of childhood. They also contain the writing elements that children enjoy: magic; fantastic creatures; excitement; danger; final safety for a worthy character. Young writers will delight in being encouraged to use these writing elements.

● Many of these story categories follow a specific format or have essential written features. There may be violent acts but these are kept within safe, and often magical, limits, as the writer knows that there must be a happy, deserved ending. There is a moral lesson to be taught as well. The writer must know in advance what this lesson will be and how the characters, setting and plot will illustrate it. Knowing and using these facts will give children useful practice in writing within a disciplined framework.

Vocabulary

Fable – a short story that is written to convey a useful moral lesson. The main characters are usually animals. A moral is written underneath the fable.
Fairy tale – a story written for, or told to, children. It usually includes elements of magic.
Legend – a traditional story about heroic characters.
Moral (of a story) – the teaching lesson addressed to the reader, written underneath a fable, and advising people how to live.
Myth – an ancient traditional story about gods or heroes.
Parable – a short story frequently linked to a religious context, written to illustrate a moral lesson or duty.

Amazing facts

Aesop's fables are the most famous fables. Aesop was a Greek storyteller who lived in the 6th century BC. These stories were only written down hundreds of years later.

Writing fiction

Common misconceptions

Myths and legends are not the same. Myths tend to be fantastical stories to explain phenomena while legends may have had their beginning in some truth that has been embellished.

Questions

Do parables have to be linked to religious teaching?
No, but they frequently are, many of them being from the Bible. However, other stories can also be parables as long as they demonstrate the virtue of dutiful behaviour.

How can the writer link the moral to the rest of the fable?
The writer should treat the animals in the story as people, depicting them as being clever and thinking like humans. In the moral, the writer should mention only people, not animals, and should emphasise the lesson that the story can teach people about how to live their lives.

Handy tip

When writing a fairy tale, bear in mind that the reader is usually a child. This will be a reminder to make the plot easy-to-follow and to include some magic.

Teaching ideas

- If the children developed fairy-tale storyboards in Chapter 1 return to these now; alternatively ask the children to create them now. Ensure they have included the relevant features, asking them to revise as necessary, and that they think about the language they use. Encourage them to comment on one another's fairy tales.

● Write a modern version of a familiar fairy tale. Characters could be more realistic (for example, a sulky Cinderella, who refuses to help her Stepmother). Situations and settings might be brought up to date: Cinderella wants to attend the school disco. What about language and lesson features? Will they be retained?

● Ask the children to help write a book of fables. Give pairs two animal characters and ask them to share ideas for short stories that teach readers how to live good lives. Suggest storyboard planning and advance writing of the morals. Create a class book.

● Link this task with the Ancient Greeks, Romans or Egyptians. Talk about natural phenomena that could have mystified ancient people. Such as: volcanic eruptions; earthquakes; droughts; tsunamis. Which natural event will the children write about? Emphasise the need for initial planning of their written myth.

● Choose and discuss a well-known legend, such as Robin Hood. Ask children to select an episode from it, plan and then write about it. (A story mountain is an effective planning frame.) Ask pairs to comment on each other's legends. Display some comments, highlighting important features of a legend.

Writing adventure and mystery stories

Subject facts

In this genre the writer will create characters that are tested, excited, frightened or puzzled, but, having struggled through, usually win in the end. The reader expects action and the stories may need greater length than usual. However, the writer must hold the attention and belief of the reader from start to finish.

Plot
This genre of story writing involves a particular order:

● **Opening:** The writer must introduce the main characters and get the story off to a quick, gripping start. Plot devices such as a warning, an unsettling discovery or urgent dialogue are effective.

- **Build-up:** In this part of the story, the writer must move the characters and action along, provide more details about the setting, build mystery and tension, and begin to create suspense.

- **Problem:** The climax of the story, when the main characters will face a problem or puzzle. The writing must be inclusive so that the reader can share the emotions of the characters. The writing must also convey strong feelings of suspense.

- **Resolution:** The writer now begins to relieve the suspense of the previous part of the story, sort out the problem or mystery, and find a way for the character's confusion or problem to be solved, for example, by bringing sudden help into the plot.

- **Ending:** The writer should return the characters to their normal state and setting. There may be talk of learning a lesson, and a character may refer back to the warning or discovery in the story opening.

Character

Characters must be interesting and credible. This involves the writer sketching characters gradually, supplying new information and revealing personality traits throughout the plot. Dialogue and actions may contribute. For example, a previously unnoticed characteristic could be revealed through something a character says, an action taken or a physical movement.

Setting

This genre needs drama and excitement, so the setting often moves between locations. Further variety may be achieved by altering the atmosphere or state of one place. For example, in *The Railway Children* the writer creates a different mood in the warm house when the family can no longer afford to heat it.

Story dividers

- **Chapters:** Chapters are efficient ways to divide long stories. Chapters let the writer choose when to 'pause'; they draw attention to changes in writing focus; and, with cliffhanger endings, may create suspense. (See Chapter 1, pages 15 and 16, for more information.)

- **Ellipses:** By using an ellipsis (…), the writer separates parts of the text and informs the reader that more is to follow.

Language features
- **Powerful verbs:** By using powerful or strong verbs (for example, *screamed* instead of *called*) the writer can add atmosphere to the story and tell the reader more about characters and their actions.

- **Time connectives:** These words appear frequently in this genre. The writer uses words and phrases such as *later, at that moment* and *afterwards* to move the action along.

- **Vague words:** In this genre, the writer makes frequent use of words that have little or no meaning: *something, somebody, it* and *someone* can add intrigue.

- **Alliteration and onomatopoeia:** Alliteration and onomatopoeia focus on the sounds of words. The writer's use of these devices can add an extra dimension of sound effects to descriptions.

- **Imagery:** Adventure and mystery stories may be long, and creating and retaining a particular atmosphere can be difficult. The writer should be aware of the reader's senses and the power of appropriate imagery, making use of similes and metaphors.

Grammar and punctuation
- **Sentence variety:** These stories may demand greater length from a writer, so a variety of long and short sentences will be important. Short sentences can increase the drama and tension of the story. Unusual sentence openings may be used, such as:
  - adverbs and adverbial phrases to begin a sentence. Informing the reader how, when or where before mentioning the action increases drama. For example: *Very suddenly, the door was yanked open from the other side.*
  - use of non-finite clauses, which involves starting the sentence with a verb. For example: *Feeling afraid, Sam clutched the key.*

- using questions more than usual. They create atmosphere as they suggest mystery and can draw the reader in, if directed at them. For example: *Someone was coming in! What could he do now?*

● **Exclamation marks:** The writer can expect to use exclamation marks more frequently than usual. This punctuation mark expresses the excitement, surprise, shock and relief that are all likely to feature strongly in this genre.

● **Dialogue:** The writer should make effective use of characters' speech. Dialogue can move action along, add to the story's atmosphere and create suspense.

Why you need to know these facts

● Adventure and mystery is a wide and popular fiction genre The children will be excited to try out their own writing skills so it is important to provide them with the correct tools.

● Grammar and punctuation are basic elements of writing. At every level, writers can make improvements. The children need to be reminded and informed of the types of words and punctuation available, and how to use them effectively.

● Even children can become set in their ways! As writers, they may not have thought of the value of varying their sentence length, type or construction.

● Language creates atmosphere. The children need to be reminded about the writer's control of the story, and hence over the reader. Figurative language and expressive sound words can make this control more effective.

Vocabulary

Adverb – a word that gives extra meaning to a verb. It may inform the reader *how*, *where*, *when* or *how often*.

Adverbial phrase – a group of words that functions in the same way as an adverb.

Dialogue – speech between two or more characters.

Ellipsis – three dots that show that something has been omitted or is incomplete.

First person – writing from a personal perspective, using *I*, *we*, *me* or *us*.

Third person – writing from the perspective of another person, using *he*, *she*, *it* or *they*.

Time connective – a linking word associated with time.

Amazing facts

Writers of this genre sometimes break the 'rule' about constructing a sentence by writing sentences of one word, for example: *Nothing*. These sentences add suspense and tension to the writing.

Common misconceptions

The chapters in a story do not have to be the same length. Writers may vary them at will.

Questions

Are adventure and mystery the same?
Most writers think that they form one genre. After all, most adventures have an element of mystery and vice versa.

Handy tip

In suitable places in the writing, refer to coldness or darkness. This will help to build tension into the story.

Teaching ideas

● Share subject ideas for a descriptive extract from an adventure or mystery story: noises outside your room or tent; an alarming thunderstorm; getting lost in fog; sharp rapping at the door. Revise writing features for suspense: some short sentences; questions; 'meaningless' words; effective descriptions. Afterwards let partners read each other's writing and use a 'response sandwich' (one positive comment, one way to improve and another positive comment) to talk about it.

● Supply an idea for the opening line of a story, for example, a warning not to open a cupboard door. Agree on important features for the early paragraphs: character introduction; dialogue; powerful verbs; some information about the setting; a hint of mystery. Ask the children to write two opening paragraphs. Share results. Do listeners want to read on?

● Show the children a reward notice for the recovery of a missing dog. Set up pairs of friends who have spotted this notice. Let them improvise two minutes of dialogue as they discuss the notice, reward and what they will do. Ask the children to write a conversation about two such characters seeing this notice. Give reminders about speech marks, powerful verbs and some exclamation marks. Can the writer imply suspense and mystery when the conversation stops?

● Put the children into groups of four or five. Talk about the different parts of a story of this genre. Recommend a story mountain as a planning structure, and share ideas for a story subject (or use an opening line from the above activities).

Encourage group discussion of each part of their story, then each member writes planning notes for one section, perhaps on a computer, before combining them for a story-mountain plan. Save the group plans for the next activity.

● Return to the previous activity's groups and plans. After group discussion and amendments, group members should write, using a computer, their part or chapter. Encourage final editing. Do chapter endings and beginnings match up? Are there cliffhangers and suspense? Does the ending refer to the opening? What about a cover, title and author names? Let the children read one another's finished, printed stories.

● Show the children an empty story-mountain plan. Provide and discuss planning notes for the opening. Ask them to complete the story mountain for the rest of the story parts. Keep these plans for the next activity.

● Return to the plans from the previous activity. Let the children talk through their proposed story with a partner. Do they want to add or amend notes? Does their story come full circle, the ending having a reference to the opening? How many chapters are needed? Let the children write their story over two to three weeks.

Writing about imagined worlds

Subject facts

All fiction deals with the imaginary, but in this genre the writer must move into completely new worlds. Through these stories, the writing aims to take the reader beyond the familiar and gain acceptance of the extraordinary. Plot and characterisation may be relevant, but it is the writer's use of setting that most transports the reader's imagination.

Fantasy
When creating fantasy, the writer describes things that are unreal or imagined and may use elements such as: extraordinary or

impossible happenings; magic; fantastic characters (elves, fairies, wizards, witches); dangerous, powerful creatures (dragons).

- **Settings:** A fantasy setting can be created through any imagined world, but the following are popular choices: parallel worlds; enchanted forests; underground places; the future. An imagined world exists initially only in the writer's imagination; their task is to share this fantasy with the reader. Descriptions, events and characters should all be used to build up the picture in the reader's head. Fantasy-story writing may move between the imagined world and the real world. In *Alice in Wonderland*, Lewis Carroll begins in the real world, as Alice sits sleepily reading a book, but quickly moves his writing to the fantasy setting of Wonderland with its strange characters and happenings when she follows a rabbit down a rabbit hole.

- **Characters:** Characters such as elves, fairies, wizards, witches, talking animals and fierce dragons are common choices. However, the writer may include ordinary human beings and through their reactions, as well as lots of description, persuade the reader to accept the fantastic characters.

- **Plot:** Plot is often not the central focus of a fantasy story – the setting and/or characters are more often the focus. Therefore the plot is usually simple and chronological in nature. When writing, it is important to consider the plot and not get bogged down by over-describing imagined worlds or characters.

- **Language:** The writer must describe the imagined world to the reader – its sights and sounds, things that may be smelled or touched, and its layout; this could include the use of imagery. In *The Hobbit*, Tolkien describes the comfortable furnishings and convenient layout of a hobbit-hole in detail. Effective choices of adjectives and adjectival phrases are essential, and the writer may even make up words.

Science fiction

In science fiction the writer must deal with imaginary, but fairly plausible, circumstances. The writer should express thoughts in a rational, credible way, and may present a story as a future development or scientific innovation.

● **Settings:** Settings can vary but popular choices include:
the future; outer space; other universes; travel between universes.

● **Characters:** Science-fiction writing often involves characters
such as aliens, humanoid robots or mutants. The writer is likely
to attribute some unusual features to the characters in the
imagined world. Distinguishing features may include colour,
voice (for example a robotic delivery or grunts) and movement.
Familiar human characters can also feature, often in unfamiliar
future-based or other-worldly settings.

● **Plot:** Science fiction often follows an adventure plot set in the
future. The plot may include devices such as flashbacks or time
travel so it may not always be chronological.

● **Language:** As with fantasy, the science fiction writer must
describe an imagined world to the reader. Hence, descriptive
detail is important, but the writing should sound rational and
seem to offer 'facts' about the world, and its location and layout.
Controlled expression is needed, but the writer may make up
words that sound appropriately scientific.

Why you need to know these facts

● All fiction writing involves using the imagination, but the genre
of imagined worlds presents focused scope for the writer's
inspiration and ideas. It is important that children are aware of
these writing opportunities.

● 'Fantasy' and 'science fiction' are labels that are often used
loosely and inaccurately. As effective fiction writers, the children
should begin to recognise some distinctions between the two.
It will increase their confidence when planning and talking about
their own writing.

● Writers can make up words! The children will gain confidence
when they realise that they can do this, and learn when and how
to make the words acceptable to the reader.

• The children should write with their reader in mind. In this genre, they have to persuade the reader to believe in complicated, yet imaginary, ideas. As writers, they must understand the importance of setting, characterisation and language in gaining the reader's trust.

Vocabulary

Fantasy (genre) – imaginary and often highly fanciful ideas in which magic may be included.
Science fiction – imaginary, but realistic, speculation about possible events, often in the future.

Common misconceptions

Fantasy and science fiction are not the same. Although both involve the imaginary, fantasy writing sets no boundaries on the imagination, whereas, science-fiction writing must have more plausible content, and be close to possibility.

Questions

Are imagined-world stories just written for children?
Fantasy is probably more popular with children, but science fiction has a large following among adults.

Handy tip

When reading this genre, pay attention to how the writer first introduces the imagined world to the reader. Try the same method in your next piece of imagined-world writing.

Teaching ideas

- Suggest a short fantasy story in which the human world leads to an imaginary world. What and where is the entrance? (A door, gate, panel or hole.) Which human character will enter? What will they see? What will happen? How will the story end? Share ideas before the children make plans. Ask them to write their first two paragraphs, the first set in the real world and the second in the imagined world. Will the reader identify easily which world is which?

- The activity above can be expanded by the children creating a detailed description of the imagined world's appearance and layout, or a labelled map showing how to return to the door leading to the human world.

- As part of a character-development activity, let the children consider their fantasy characters. Are they unreal enough? Is another magical element or special effect needed? Would a made-up word enhance the fantasy? Encourage the children to amend their plans as required before they write two paragraphs with descriptive detail about a fantasy character's appearance and actions.

- Ask the children to imagine a new planet. Encourage them to make notes as they visualise it: appearance; inhabitants; relationship with our planet. They must keep this picture in their mind while they write a paragraph or two about the arrival on Earth of some of this planet's inhabitants. Let partners act as each other's reader. Do they find each other's science-fiction writing credible? Encourage constructive criticism.

- In pairs, ask the children to swap one of their written character descriptions. Ask each child to draw the inhabitant of their partner's imagined world. Does the picture look how the writer envisaged?

- Ask the children to create a glossary of about 20 made-up words that could be used in their science-fiction story. The words need to have credibility in order for the reader to take the writing seriously.

Writing stories about real issues

Subject facts

In this genre, the writer confronts true-to-life situations. Hence, the writing is realistic and may deal with issues that present difficulties in the reader's life. The medium of fiction allows the writer to approach these issues sensitively.

Realistic lives

Here the writer demonstrates awareness that life is not always happy or easy. By including subjects such as parental divorce, poverty, or being fostered or adopted in a story, the writer can show empathy with the reader. Jacqueline Wilson has used these issues extensively in her fiction writing.

Sensitive issues

Some issues that seem too difficult to be faced by children may nevertheless have to be confronted in real life – disability and death are examples. The writer may help the young reader by approaching such issues carefully, and using characters, dialogue and plot as a means of guiding the reader towards acceptance.

Moral dilemmas

Issues in these stories may present a character with a difficult decision to make. By creating such plots, the writer should provoke the reader into thinking about the decisions they would make. It could include issues such as jealousy, divided loyalty or honesty. The writer needs to build up the story using varied sentence length and a cliffhanger when the dilemma is reached, emphasising the it by using words such as *may*, *maybe* or *perhaps*.

Why you need to know these facts

● This is an interesting genre for child writers as it lets them use the problems of modern life, many of which may be relevant to them, in their writing. Such freedom may inspire further writing for many of them.

● It is important that the children know that there is not a clear distinction between the themes of fiction and non-fiction writing. Some children may not have thought of writing stories that raise realistic issues in this way.

● Children need to be reminded to write with the reader in mind. In this genre, they can use realism to attract and involve their reader, and they can create characters' problems and solutions to help the reader.

● This genre can help the writer as well as the reader. A difficult issue affecting the writer may become part of the story. The writer may use the solution created for the story's dilemma as a springboard to finding a solution in real life.

Vocabulary

Dilemma – a problem that presents a choice between two difficult alternatives.
Issue – important subject or topic.
Moral (dilemma) – concerned with goodness or badness of character, and the distinction between right and wrong.
Realism – showing life as it is.
Social – concerned with people's relationships in society.

Amazing facts

Jacqueline Wilson is a children's author who commonly writes fiction about real issues. One of her books is sold every 30 seconds in Britain. In ten years, her books were borrowed 16 million times from British libraries!

Common misconceptions

Real issues do not have to make sad books. The writer can use humour, yet be touching and provoke the reader to think about the issues afterwards.

Questions

Do stories about real issues have to be serious?
No! Jacqueline Wilson manages to be very funny, yet also thought-provoking, while her characters reassure the reader that there are other people coping with the same issues of life.

Handy tip

Make regular stops during writing to read your story.
Check that your characters seem true-to-life in their reactions to difficult issues.

Teaching ideas

● Present a scenario: the usual person is starring in the school Christmas concert; a group of children, as a joke, 'misplace' her dress, intending to replace it after a day or two. The situation spirals out of control! The girl phones home; her parents are involved; the school takes the matter seriously; an investigation and search is underway. The guilty children panic. Put the children into groups to improvise dialogue at different stages. This will help them to write more realistic speech.

● Outline writing ideas for part of a story: the main character has a group of friends; the group starts to exclude and bully someone; the main character faces a dilemma. Ask the children to write two or three paragraphs of this story, perhaps in the first person, stopping at the cliffhanger dilemma. Put the children into small groups to read their work to one another. Do the listeners understand the moral dilemma? What are the two difficult choices? Is the writing realistic?

● Let the children choose a social issue: divorce; unusual family units; living in care; unemployment. As writers, through their fiction they can help a reader coping with the issue. Ask the children to plan and write a relevant short story. Emphasise the need for realism, so that the reader believes in the characters and the plot.

● Talk about sensitive issues: the death of someone close; caring for a parent; having a disability. Their reader is coping with this issue. As writers, they want that imagined reader to be a main character in their story. The story should show awareness of the difficulties faced by the main character, but, as illustrated by the characters, dialogue and plot, some happiness. Let the children plan and write the short story.

Writing historical fiction

Subject facts

In these stories, the modern writer returns to the past to re-create a former time period. The dialogue, year references, way of life, dress, transport and housing must all be compatible to the year chosen for the story setting, so preparatory research is important.

● **Setting:** The setting is in the past; it could be in any period but specific detail will be required. Writing stories that involve other cultures demands background knowledge from the writer. The story is fiction, but it must be credible. The setting may be a different country, so it is important that names and references to beliefs and ways of life make the reader feel comfortable. Similarly, if the writer makes customs and traditions important to the plot, the reader must be able to accept their credibility.

● **Plot:** The plot usually centres around an event that happened in the past. Sometimes the story may start in the present and flash back to a different time period. It could form an adventure story or mystery, it could be based around something that really happened, creating a fiction to 'fill in the gap' – this is what Berlie Doherty does in *Street Child* where she tells the story of Jim Jarvis who led Dr Barnardo to found his charity.

● **Character:** The characters should be appropriate to the setting in the way they speak and in description. For example, what they are wearing should reflect the time period.

● **Language:** The writing should match its setting, plot and characters, so historical fiction is often written in the third person and past tense. However, historical stories can provide an effective opportunity to adopt the voice of a character and, as in a diary, write in the first person. Writing in this way, as the first person narrator, the author is likely to make some use of the present tense. The writer can sometimes have a voice in a story, which can be an effective way of forming a relationship with the reader. The writer may portray two time periods within the same story. This needs care with period references, characters' dialogue and their way of living. The writing should reflect the time period it is set in: this could involve using old-fashioned words or grammatical structures. Writers may use the device of a character telling a story or dreaming to move the story back in time. New chapters, or even font or writing-style changes, are other ways for the writer to change time. In *Carrie's War*, the first chapter is in the present day, the second has slipped back to the Second World War.

Why you need to know these facts

● These types of stories are different and quite specialised. As writers, the children may need to put themselves in another time and place. They will need to know how to write successfully.

● Reminders about verb tense are always helpful to a writer. Some children may still confuse first and third person in their writing. Revision of the difference will be helpful.

● As writers, the children may never have thought of putting their own voice into their story. Knowing how this can be done, and its effect on the reader, will add to their writing toolbox.

Vocabulary

Culture – the behaviour or beliefs characteristic of a particular social, ethnic or age group.
Custom – usual way of behaving.
Historical – belonging to the past.
Tradition – belief, opinion or custom passed down from previous generations.

Handy tip

When writing a story about a different time or culture, research names for your characters so that you create convincing people for the reader.

Teaching ideas

● Ask the children to open their story with an elderly person. They should introduce and describe this main character – their age, interests, home and family. The writing should be mainly in the present tense and use the third person. The children are going to continue the story, but move back in time to the childhood of their main character. How will they join the pieces of writing? How will they indicate the time change to the reader? A new chapter, a space, an ellipsis (…) would all be effective.

● During work on a history topic encourage the children to imagine they live during that time period and to create a personal character profile.

● Ask the children to interview older family members about what life was like when they were growing up. The children could use their notes from the interview as inspiration for a story.

Resources

Recommended sources of fiction:
All of these books provide inspiring examples of fiction writing.
The Boy in the Striped Pyjamas by John Boyne (David Fickling Books)
Woof! by Allan Ahlberg (Puffin Books)
My Friend Walter by Michael Morpurgo (Egmont Books)
The Magic Finger by Roald Dahl (Puffin Books)
Carrie's War by Nina Bawden (Puffin Modern Classics)
The Railway Children by E Nesbit (Puffin Classics)
From Out of the Shadows by Jamila Gavin (Egmont Books)
Spy Dog Captured! by Andrew Cope (Puffin Books)
Pigeon Post by Arthur Ransome (Random House Children's Books)
Emil and the Detectives by Erich Kästner (Random House Children's Books)
Atticus the Storyteller's 100 Greek Myths by Lucy Coats (Orion Children's Books)
The Story of Tracy Beaker by Jacqueline Wilson (Doubleday Corgi Yearling Books)
Charlotte's Web by EB White (Puffin Modern Classics)
Harry Potter and the Prisoner of Azkaban by JK Rowling (Bloomsbury Publishing)

Further reading:
How to Teach Story Writing at KS1 by Pie Corbett (Letts)
How to Teach Fiction Writing at KS2 by Pie Corbett (Letts)
How to Teach Writing Across the Curriculum by Sue Palmer (Routledge Publishers)
Write out of the Classroom: How to use the outdoors to inspire and create amazing writing by Colin Macfarlane (Routledge Publishers)

Non-fiction

The scope of non-fiction writing is vast and there are numerous genres. Nevertheless, the writing style choices may be restricted as the writer is working with facts, not imagination. This must be evident in the chosen language and appearance of the finished text.

Before writing non-fiction

Subject facts

Planning and preparation

● **Research:** The writer's first task is to find out the facts of the subject to be written about. Sources can include: books, the internet, first-hand knowledge and interviews of other people.

● **Note-making:** Preparatory writing of the research should be in note form. Care must be taken at this stage to note the correct spelling of technical words or proper names. Quotes may also be noted: for these, the exact words used are needed. The notes should have the following features:

- will be understood later by the writer
- correct facts
- words and phrases, not sentences
- abbreviations
- careful recording of technical words, proper names, date or quotes
- chronology of events
- organisational devices
- layout that will later be helpful to the writer
- signs or symbols.

● **Genre:** The writer must decide in advance on the appropriate genre of non-fiction writing, and then follow the writing conventions for that genre. (Each genre has a separate section in this chapter.) However, it is important to be aware that writers do not always keep to one genre; a text can be a mixture of genres.

● **Pictorial plans:** Pictures and diagrams can be helpful formats when preparing to write some non-fiction texts. In this plan, the writer has prepared information in the form of a pictorial flow chart to explain the development of a sunflower:

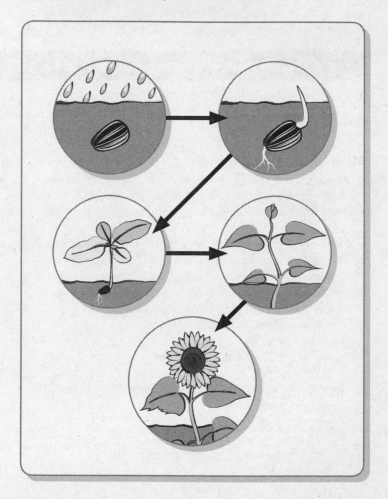

In the diagram below, the writer has used a cyclical flow chart, with brief notes to plan an explanatory text about the process of an acorn becoming a tree:

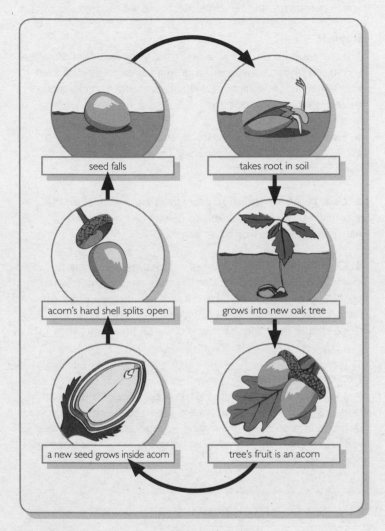

seed falls	takes root in soil
acorn's hard shell splits open	grows into new oak tree
a new seed grows inside acorn	tree's fruit is an acorn

Writing

● **Style:** Non-fiction writing style is often matter-of-fact and to the point. The tone may be formal or businesslike, with an emphasis by the writer on being understood. In other cases, for example a recount, the style may be friendly and even conversational.

● **Language:** The writer may expect to use fewer words in non-fiction writing. Unlike fiction, extra descriptions and figurative language are not always appropriate. Language may be formal and impersonal, with the correct technical words used.

Layout

The aim must be clarity. The writer's task is to impart information to the reader as clearly as possible. In addition to dividing text into sentences, paragraphs and chapters, the writer may use these organisational devices:

● **Headings and subheadings:** The writer usually places these above a paragraph, hence informing the reader in advance of the paragraph's content.

● **Lists:** In many non-fiction genres, it is conventional to list information. The writer is likely to demarcate the list items with numbers, letters or bullet points.

● **Organisation:** Organisation of information is important in non-fiction texts. The order of the writing may be dictated by the chronology of the facts, division into themes, order of importance, or an alphabetical, numerical or physical order (for example, facts about the body may be presented from head to toe).

Pictorial elements

In non-fiction texts, the writer often makes use of pictures and diagrams. However, their purpose must be to inform and provide evidence in support of the writing – not to add an imaginative illustration. Labelled diagrams can be an important part of some non-fiction texts.

Why you need to know these facts

● The writer should approach non-fiction texts differently. There is a definite distinction between the imaginary world of fiction and the actual world of fact: the children must alter the way they write. They will need to be aware of this.

● The children may easily lapse into writing fiction. As writers, they need to understand their different task: this writing does not only have to be credible (as, for example, the fiction of a historical story); it also has to be correct (as, for example, in a non-fiction historical report).

● All writing benefits from planning, but non-fiction text may require both knowledge and research. The children must know that there is often considerable preparatory work to be done before they should plan the layout and write the text.

● Writers can make greater use of pictures in non-fiction texts. However, children are easily distracted by the opportunity for imaginative, attractive illustration. As non-fiction writers, they will need to know that their picture requires an informative purpose.

Vocabulary

Bullet point – a small dot or square that is placed before an item or phrase in a list.
Subheading – a further heading placed below the main heading or headline.

Teaching ideas

● Point out a piece on non-fiction writing on display. Could the writer have made more effective use of headings, subheadings, lists, bullet points, diagrams or pictures? Ask the children to discuss, in small groups, how they would change the layout and presentation for a different reader. Let groups present their ideas.

● Let the children talk to a partner about note-making. Suggest they use a heading and bullet points to list important features of notes. Compare results and agree on a list.

● Remind the children about a recent class trip and ask them to make notes on what they did. Keep these notes for a later activity.

● Talk about a particular science topic, such as space or local wildlife. Explain that they need to write a report on this topic. Ask them to plan and list their order of work. Then identify two or three websites and books they could use for information.

● Talk about the water cycle; discuss how the process forms a continuous cycle. Ask the children to create a cyclical flow chart, containing pictures or notes showing the information. Ask them to keep this as a plan for future writing in a later section.

Writing reports

Subject facts

In a report, the task is to describe the way things are. The writer may use this non-fiction form to: describe human behaviour; account for classifications; report on the range of an item's use, functions and qualities. The scope is wide.

Structure
● **Content order:** The writer needs a clear opening statement and introductory paragraph, telling the reader the subject of the report. Subsequent facts are usually presented in a non-chronological, random order. For example, in a report on healthy eating, the writer may place a paragraph with the subheading *Vegetables* before or after one with the subheading *Fruit*.

● **Sentences:** In order to add authority to the report, the writer should expect to use some longer and complex sentences, and aim to punctuate them in a way that is both appropriate and helpful to the reader.

Language
● **Verbs:** Reports should be written in the appropriate person and tense, usually the third-person present tense. The writer may make some use of the passive voice, as in this example from a non-chronological report on storing food:

*The life of dairy products **may be extended** by cool storage.*

- **Vocabulary:** The writer's purpose is to provide accurate information. Therefore, it is essential to use the correct technical words for the subject.

Style

The style or tone of the writing should be impersonal. The writer may make some use of the passive voice in order to achieve this. (See Verbs above.)

Layout

The writer's aim must be to help the reader access information. To this end, sections, paragraphs, headings and subheadings are likely to be used in a report: they act as signposts. In addition, the writer may decide that a picture or diagram will add information.

Why you need to know these facts

- Report writing covers a limitless number of subjects and contexts. Writing a report will be a necessary life skill often expected by an employer. The children must start to acquire these writing skills needed for the future.

- The children need to know why they are writing! They must recognise the purpose of this genre: to inform, not to entertain. Knowing this, will affect the way the children write and present their reports.

- Layout is integral to this genre. As writers, the children must keep their reader in mind. They will realise that their headings, subheadings and punctuation are signposts to the reader, and will think more carefully how they word and where they place them.

- The passive voice is not easy to understand, so gradual introduction is ideal. Report writing lets children begin to use this verb form. They will start to recognise the formal authority that it can bring to their writing.

Vocabulary

Chronological order – following the order in which events occur in time.

Complex sentence – a sentence that has a main clause and one or more subordinate clauses.

Non-chronological order – not organised according to the order in which events occur in time.

Passive – the form of a verb in which the subject of the sentence has the verb's action done to it, for example: *The bacteria are destroyed by high temperatures.* The passive form creates an impersonal style.

Report – a text written to inform a newspaper or magazine reader, often about recent events.

Amazing facts

Reports seem an unlikely place for questions, but these can be an effective choice of headings and subheadings by the writer.

Common misconceptions

Adjectives do not have to be omitted from reports, but they do need to be factual.

Teaching ideas

● Display a sentence that uses an active verb: *The boy opened the cage.* Identify and underline in different colours: the subject (*the boy*); the active verb (*opened*); the receiving object (*the cage*). Demonstrate converting the verb into the passive voice: *The cage*

was opened by the boy. Discuss what has happened. Give the children other active sentences to change into passive ones.

● Decide on a curriculum area in geography or science and let the children choose the focus for a non-chronological report: for example, the state of the country's flood defences. Discuss the preparation needed. Can they identify: what they already know; what they need to find out? Let the children do their preparatory work and write their notes, including technical vocabulary. Once planned, discuss appropriate writing features and layout for their reports and then let them write the non-chronological report.

● Suggest to the children that they have been asked to write about a particular history topic, such as the Industrial Revolution or the evacuees of the Second World War. Encourage them to research their topic and plan their writing. Can they identify two or three websites and books they could use for information? Can the children plan and list their order of work?

● Return to the notes from the previous task. Let the children plan their layout. What headings and subheadings will they write? Will they use questions? Would these be accurate signposts for the reader? Remind them to use the past tense, and to be aware of chronology when needed. Let the children write their report. Is it impersonal enough? Encourage a style check and final editing before printing.

Writing a recount

Subject facts

A recount is a retelling. The writer provides the reader with an account of something that has already happened. Written in the first or third person, this genre should be used when focusing on an occasion and people. The writer may expect to cover this range:

• an eyewitness account of an historic event
• a personal experience
• local events or incidents.

Structure

● **Content order:** The writer must orientate the reader with an opening statement or paragraph that establishes the context of the recount: who, when and where. After that, events should be written in chronological order ending with a closing statement.

● **Sentences:** The writer should construct sentences that are appropriate and helpful to the reader., considering the audience is important.

Language

● **Time connectives:** These are important to both the writer and reader of a recount: the writer can sequence the past events accurately; the reader is reminded of the order of events. Useful examples include *while*, *once* and *in the end*.

● **Verbs:** Recounts should be written in the past tense, as they are about events that have already happened, so verbs should be used accordingly. A recount may be written in the first or third person, depending on the author's involvement in the events.

● **Vocabulary:** The writer's purpose is to provide accurate information that can be understood by the reader. Although essential, technical words must be used, other vocabulary should be selected with the identified reader in mind. For example, this extract is from a newspaper recount of a football match:

> *Last night's international youth match between Holland and England was a disaster. No goals and two red cards left both sets of fans disgruntled.*

The same match is reported in a children's magazine:

> *The football game between Holland and England was not enjoyable. Each side had a player sent off and no goals were scored. The fans were unhappy.*

Style

The style or tone of the writing should be appropriate for the intended audience. The selection of the first or third person will affect the tone that the writer wants to convey to the reader.

Layout

The writer may provide an illustration if it will be helpful to the reader.

Why you need to know these facts

● Non-fiction text genres can be easily confused. The children need to become familiar with the different names and writing characteristics.

● A recount has a 'tidy', logical structure, comfortable for a writer to use. The children will find many occasions to write in this genre, for example, if asked to represent the team and provide information about yesterday's netball match.

● The children will add to their knowledge of the interaction between writer and reader, particularly how the reader influences the writer's selection of words, punctuation and sentence construction. This understanding will extend the children's skills as writers.

● Recounts and reports are closely related, so it is important to be clear about the main difference: recounts retell events whereas reports describe the way things are.

Vocabulary

Orientation – opening statement sentence(s) that sets the scene for the rest of the recount.
Recount – a written retelling of an event or series of events.

Amazing facts

A writer always uses a recount to retell events, but the purpose is sometimes to entertain the reader, not just inform.

Common misconceptions

Recounts do not have to be formal pieces of text. The writer may use a 'chatty' tone for a young reader, for example:

I really liked the Roman Armoury. The curator let me hold a Roman sword!

Teaching ideas

● Model opening sentences that orientate the reader by answering: Who? Where? When? For example: *Last summer holiday our family stayed with my grandparents in Devon.* Ask the children to decide on the subject of a recount about their own family. Let them make notes about what happened, in chronological order, and then talk a partner through their notes. Save the notes for the next activity.

● Return to the notes from the previous activity. Encourage partner discussion as the children list important writing features for their recount. Share ideas and agree on a list, the children drawing a tick box next to each feature. Let the children write their recount, assess it and tick the box of each feature included. What have they omitted? Encourage editing before they settle on a text that ticks all the boxes!

● Ask the children to write notes about a recent school trip. Let partners talk through their notes to each other and then ask them to use their notes to write a recount of the trip. Point out that the recount will describe their personal experience of the trip, so not everyone's experiences will be the same. Emphasise writing in the first person, and ensuring that essential words are correct. It will be read by children of their age: what tone will they try to create in their writing?

● Talk about a historic event: the arrival of Florence Nightingale at Scutari hospital; Mary Seacole's return from the Crimea;

Elizabeth I's visit to Kenilworth Castle. Ask the children to do research and make notes before writing an eyewitness memory of the event. Remind them to use past-tense verbs.

● Use partner and class discussion about a local event or incident: the carnival; a rescue operation when the river overflowed. Ask the children to write a recount. Emphasise the need for past-tense verbs, chronological order, and a focus on individuals or groups.

Writing an explanation

Subject facts

In this genre, the writer has to explain a process or tell the reader how something works. The writing should provide an answer to the questions *How?* and *Why?*

Structure
● **Content order:** The title is often a question beginning with *How… ?* or *Why… ?* The topic must be further introduced in an opening statement. The main explanation should follow, written in a series of steps.

● **Sentences:** In order to convey an authoritative tone, the writer should expect to use some longer and complex sentences. However, style must match the comprehension level of the reader, so when writing for a younger reader, the author's sentence construction may be simplified.

Language
● **Time connectives:** These are sequential connections and should be used by the writer to confirm the order of the steps in the process.

● **Verbs:** Explanation texts are usually written in the third-person present tense and the writer may make use of passive verbs.

● **Causal connectives:** The explanation writer should expect to make frequent use of causal connectives. These cause and effect phrases emphasise the relationship between an action and its result. For example: *If the circuit is complete,* **then** *the bulb lights up.*

● **Vocabulary:** The writer must include technical vocabulary, for example, *circuit* in the text above.

Style

The writer often needs to adopt an impersonal tone so that attention is paid to the information. Writing is usually in the third person, describing the subject of the text. Nevertheless, the author may address the reader directly by using questions that encourage the reader to think about the information being explained. When necessary, the passive voice can help the writer achieve a detached, authoritative style.

Layout

● **Organisational devices:** The writer's aim must be to help the reader understand. Therefore, headings, subheadings, numbers and letters may be used to make the text clearer.

● **Diagrams:** These are usually a helpful addition to an explanation text. Furthermore, the writer should consider adding labels to the diagram, and must make clear in the text which diagram is being referred to.

Why you need to know these facts

● Children need to know the structure of an explanation, to know the organisational devices available to the writer, and to recognise the importance of giving information to the reader in a series of steps.

● The word *sequential* is often used to refer to an explanation's step-by-step order. The children need to know that 'sequential connectives' may also be called 'time connectives'. Possessing this alternative, more precise vocabulary will allow them to speak with informed authority about their intended writing.

• 'Causal connection' or 'cause-and-effect connectives' may be new terms. As writers, the children should add the synonymous labels, examples, and practical application to their knowledge of writing and the skills at their disposal.

• The children's writing will improve as they become more adept at constructing complex sentences. Knowing, for example, when to use pairs of commas to embed clauses within their sentences will add to their confidence.

Vocabulary

Causal connective – a linking phrase that confirms cause or effect.
Sequential connective – a linking phrase that confirms the order of events. It may also be referred to as a 'time connective'.

Teaching ideas

• Provide unpunctuated complex sentences for the children to add commas to, to demarcate the subordinate clause. Then give the children simple sentences with only a main clause and ask them to embed a subordinate clause in each, using two commas.

• Provide ten short simple sentences on a particular science topic. Ask the children to create complex sentences by pairing the clauses using causal connectives, for example: *therefore; because; so; if…then; in order that; as a result.*

• After the children have made their flow charts (see Before writing non-fiction), talk about converting them into explanation texts. Remind them about a 'How/Why' title, the passive voice, the present tense and connectives. Agree on a list of essential technical words before the children begin their writing.

• Explain a process verbally, for example, how sounds are made. Ask the children to make notes, then to write an explanation from the notes. Use paired assessment: Is the writing impersonal enough? Are verb voice and tense appropriate? Would a diagram be helpful?

● Remind the children about a process that they are familiar with, for example, sending an email. Encourage initial planning and checking of technical words before they write an explanation for this process. Let small groups review one another's texts. Suggest a response sandwich: a favourable comment; an idea for improvement; another favourable comment.

Writing instructions

Subject facts

In an instructional text, the writer's purpose is to teach the reader how to do or make something. This form of text needs to be written with particular clarity.

Structure
● **Content order:** A title should tell the reader the aim of the text. After that, a list of the equipment needed should be written. The *What to do* section follows and forms the bulk of the writing.

● **Chronological order:** The main text should be written in the form of a series of chronological steps.

● **Sentences:** The writer's aim must be clarity, so short, command sentences are frequently used. Adjectives and adverbs should be used only when their meaning is required, not for interesting description.

Language
● **Time connectives:** Time words, such as *then* and *now*, are an effective way to support the chronology of the text.

● **Verbs:** Text should be written in the present tense. Imperative verbs are essential, the writer aiming to place them at, or close to, the beginning of a sentence.

- **Vocabulary:** In this non-fiction genre, the writer is not only imparting information, but also teaching the reader how to achieve a stated purpose. Correct names must be used.

Layout

- **Organisational devices:** The use of boxes, bullet points and symbols can make the text's meaning clear. Subheadings, short lines and bullet points are useful for dividing text, particularly the chronological stages of the instructions. Numbers and letters may be used to emphasise correct order, and the writer may draw attention to important words with bold letters and capitals.

- **Pictures:** Illustrations and diagrams can be an effective way for the writer to make the meaning or outcome of the instructions clear.

Why you need to know these facts

- This genre is particularly exacting in the demands made on the writer for clearly expressed, accurate information. The children need to appreciate this emphasis on clarity.

- Imperative verbs are integral to instruction texts. The children will need to: use this second-person verb form in their sentences; know where best to position them; be aware that they should not include the pronoun *you* before the verb form, but merely let the reader understand the command as being addressed to them.

- Revision of time connectives is always useful. When using them in an instruction text, the children will create ordered links between sentences and between sections, and so help the reader to understand their text.

- The children may confuse instructions with explanations. The writer may deal with the same topic, and using *How* as the title's first word may further confuse. It is important that the children recognise the distinctions between the two text types.

Vocabulary

Command sentence – an alternative name for an imperative sentence. It tells the reader what to do.

Imperative verb – the second-person form of the verb that gives a command. The pronoun *you* is not written, merely understood.

Common misconceptions

Not every sentence in an instruction text has to be a command sentence. Nevertheless, the writer should expect most sentences to be in this format.

Handy tip

Put yourself in the reader's place and test your instructions. If you cannot follow them successfully, the instructions need rewriting.

Teaching ideas

● Practise writing imperative verbs by providing statement and question sentences to convert into written command sentences. Share results. What changes were necessary? (Changing the verb's form and possibly tense; removing a pronoun; altering final punctuation.) Was the new sentence shorter?

● Give the children a written instructional text with many faults: incorrect use of imperative verbs; too few command sentences; wordiness; poor layout; no diagrammatic support. Let the children rewrite the instructions. Working on a computer would allow for thoughtful changes.

● Ask the children to write a school instructional text: *What to do in the event of a fire; How to summon help for a playground accident*. Point out that the instructions are for times of stress and their readers may be children. Short, clear sentences and helpful layout are essential.

● Set a writing task for instructions that involve some simultaneous activities. For example: some computer operations; a cookery recipe; a swimming stroke. Point out some writing pitfalls and discuss how the usual writing sequence may lead to the reader making an error. Encourage partner discussion about how the writer can make the instructions clear. After writing, let partners assess each other's texts.

Discussion texts

Subject facts

This is a text in which all sides of an issue are presented. The writer's task is to create a balanced text, by providing arguments from a number of viewpoints.

Structure
● **Opening:** The text should begin with a clear opening statement of the issue involved.

● **Evidence:** The opening statement must be followed by arguments for and against. The writer usually supports these with evidence.

● **Conclusion:** The writer finishes with a summary of the points made and a concluding statement.

● **Sentences:** A discussion text needs to hold the reader's attention. The writer should vary sentence length and type, and include questions addressed to the reader. Some sentences should be complex, with sophisticated construction and punctuation.

Language

- **Connectives:** The writer should use connectives to make smooth links between arguments, sentences and paragraphs. Logical connectives are likely to feature strongly, as they provide rational links between arguments. For example:

  Pandas cope badly with abrupt changes in environment.
  Consequently, *when brought here, they rarely breed.*

- **Verbs:** Discussion texts are written in the present tense, which allows the writer to convey the strength and urgency of viewpoints.

- **Vocabulary:** The writer should avoid references to specific people, but instead make general references with words such as *individuals*, *they* and *people*. Language choice is very important; it can affect the tone of the argument and its effect on the reader. For example, a connective may have the effect of strengthening or opposing an argument. Here, *Consequently* introduces a supportive argument; *However* introduces an opposing argument:

  Pandas cope badly with abrupt changes in environment.
  Consequently, *when brought here, they rarely breed.*
  However, *some zoos achieve considerable success with well-designed enclosures.*

- **Rhetorical questions:** This type of question requires no answer. By using this language device, the writer engages the reader in the issue. It is an effective writing technique.

Style

The writer should try to achieve a formal tone. Word selection, punctuation and some impersonal language, such as general references (*many people*) will all contribute to this style.

Why you need to know these facts

- This is a useful writing genre as it lends itself to many areas of the curriculum, such as history and geography topics. For example: *Did the Roman invaders help Britain?*

Was Henry VIII good for the monarchy? Should the high street be closed to traffic?

● Discussion texts are interesting, yet demanding, to write. There is a specified format, verb tense, and a careful use of connectives required. The children will need to know and practise these techniques if they are to write successfully in this genre.

● There is tactical use of language in this genre. For example, the writer's subtle use of apparently benign connectives, *therefore* and *however*, can alter the weight of an argument: the first implies logical conclusion; the second implies opposition. Knowing this will remind the children of the power of their word selection.

Vocabulary

Balance – a weighing of arguments.
Discussion text – writing that presents all sides of an issue.
Rhetorical question – a question that does not really need a reply.

Handy tip

As the writer, ask yourself: *Will this completed text give the reader a balanced view of opinions on this issue and help them reach a decision?* The answer should be yes.

Teaching ideas

● Give the children two connectives: *consequently* and *but*. Ask them to write one in this gap: *It often pours with rain on Sports Day __ many children have a cold.* Discuss the results; point out that *consequently* makes catching a cold seem the logical result of a wet Sports Day and that *but* makes Sports Day rain and catching a cold seem unconnected.

- List these connectives: *nevertheless; as a result; but; however; therefore; on the other hand; consequently; because*. Ask the children to write them in two equal groups, under these headings: *Connectives that support the preceding argument; Connectives that present the other side*. Compare results. Ask children to make up pairs of sentences for a partner to link with one of the connectives. Encourage paired discussion about the effect on meaning.

- Choose an issue relevant to current history or geography work. Use partner and class discussion to identify important arguments. Ask the children to plan the structure and content for a discussion text on the subject, perhaps using a 'for and against' grid. What evidence will they include? Keep the plans for later use.

- Return to the plans from the previous activity. Encourage the children to note some useful vocabulary they will use, such as: general words to refer to people; connectives and places to use them; the opening and closing statements. Ask the children to write their discussion texts.

- Ask the children to list writing features they would expect to use in a discussion text. Share results as a class and agree on a final version. Use this to create a tick-list for self- and peer-assessment of their texts. Encourage partners to discuss their results.

- Choose an issue relevant to the children's lives. For example: mobile phones in school; uniform. Let partners discuss the issue and decide on for and against arguments. Ask the children to work on their own evidence and plans before writing their discussion text. Organise groups of four to assess one another's texts using a response sandwich: one good comment; one area for improvement; another good comment.

Persuasive writing

In this genre, the writer's task is to argue a particular point of view and to persuade the reader to agree with that viewpoint.

Structure
- **Title:** The title may be written in the form of a question. For example: *Does the new superstore wreck our town?*

- **Opening:** The writer should begin with a paragraph that introduces the issue and states the view taken.

- **Arguments and evidence:** It must be made clear in the text that one side of the issue is being supported. The ensuing arguments then need the support of evidence, reasons and statistics. The writer should select which facts to use and consider how to use them to be persuasive. Opposing views may be briefly mentioned, but only with the intention of disproving them or to demonstrate the reasonableness of the main viewpoint.

- **Ending:** The concluding paragraph should consist of a summary of some main points and an emphatic restatement of the view supported.

Language
- **Connectives:** The writer needs to make effective use of connectives to create smooth links between arguments, sentences and paragraphs. Logical connectives are likely to be used frequently – they help the writer build arguments by demonstrating rational links between points and evidence.

- **Verbs:** The present tense is the effective choice. It is best able to convey the strength, urgency and passion of the writer's viewpoint.

- **Vocabulary:** General references, with words such as *individuals, they* and *people* may be used. Language may be passionate, emotive and even manipulative, as the writer tries to gain the reader's agreement. Varied vocabulary is important to hold reader attention and the writer can make convincing use of phrases such as: *For your information…*; *It is a fact that…*; *It is important that…*; *There is evidence to show…*

● **Sentences:** The writer should vary sentence length and type, and include questions addressed directly to the reader. Some sentences should be complex, with sophisticated construction and punctuation. By demonstrating this control, the writer suggests a similarly skilful thought process. This is persuasive.

● **Rhetorical questions:** By using this language device, the writer can catch the reader's attention and manipulate their thinking. It can be a useful persuasive technique.

Style

The writer should try to achieve a formal tone. Word selection, punctuation and some impersonal language such as general references (*some people; they; individuals*) will all contribute to this style.

Why you need to know these facts

● The children must understand the importance of facts in a persuasive text. By writing statistics, numbers and details to support an argument, they are more likely to persuade the reader of the validity of their viewpoint.

● It is easy to confuse persuasion and discussion texts. As writers, the children will need to have identified their essential difference: persuasion supports one side; discussion adopts an overview.

● There are important language points in persuasive writing. Varied vocabulary, thoughtful use of connectives and well-structured sentences are skills that all writers need to keep practising.

Vocabulary

Persuasive text – writing that argues a particular point of view.
Rhetorical question – a question that does not really need
a reply.

Amazing facts

Everyday life brings exposure to numerous examples of
persuasive writing: advertisements! (Advertisements are
examined closely in Chapter 6, 'Media'.)

Common misconceptions

Persuasion texts and discussion texts are not the same:
persuasive writing argues a particular point of view; discussion
texts present arguments from a number of viewpoints.

Handy tip

Before you start writing a persuasive text, make a list of strong
sentence openers. This will ensure varied vocabulary.

Teaching ideas

● There has been talk of ending educational trips. In small
groups, ask the children to discuss the points for and against
outings. Ask them to adopt a viewpoint and write a persuasive
text, perhaps in the form of a letter to be sent to parents.

● Consider a history topic with controversial events or figures, for example, Henry VIII's treatment of his wives. Is Henry fit to remain as King? Discuss arguments for and against. Let the children plan and write a persuasive text, either for or against, from the viewpoint of someone alive at the same time.

● Discuss a topic related to school organisation. For example: *Should there be four school terms instead of three?* Ask the children to take a view and plan and write a piece of persuasive writing. Encourage them to present their arguments and evidence in an impersonal way, and to make little reference to themselves.

● Ask the children to look at a discussion text they have written and this time choose one viewpoint: for or against. Rewrite it as a persuasive text and compare the features and effect.

Writing biographies and autobiographies

Subject facts

A biography and an autobiography are both life-stories. In a biography, the writer writes about someone else's life. In an autobiography, the writer is both the subject and author of the text.

Biography structure
● **Opening:** The opening sentence must hook the reader. The writer may choose a device such as a rhetorical question, a brief summary of the subject's life or a straightforward entry into the beginning of the subject's life.

● **Chronological order:** The writer's task in a biography is twofold: to recount key events in the subject's life and to give the reader an insight into the subject's character. The main events and achievements of the subject should be provided in chronological order; paragraphs are the writer's means of separating and sequencing these events. Some general, explanatory paragraphs including information about people linked to the subject should be written to provide the reader with detail.

● **Conclusion:** In the final part of the text, the writer should sum up the subject's character and mention their importance in their profession or field. A personal opinion by the writer may be written, along with a comment on how the subject is likely to be remembered.

Biography language

● **Time connectives:** The writer will find time connectives an effective way to support the chronology of the text. Having a stock of varied linking phrases and words is essential, for example: *Eventually…; In the year…; Later in life…; Early on…*

● **Verbs:** The author should expect to write in the past tense. However, if the subject is still alive, there may be occasion to deviate from this. The third person will be used throughout.

Biography style

The tone of the text is often quite formal and impersonal, with the writer seeming detached from the subject. Use of the third person is important, and the passive voice a useful verb form when trying to achieve formality in the text.

Autobiography structure

● **Chronological order:** The writer should recount key events in their own life. These events should usually be in chronological order, but the writer may choose to deviate from this at times. Family, friends and acquaintances should be written about, and the writer must expect to reveal personal feelings, ideals, aspirations and beliefs.

● **Conclusion:** In the final part of the text, the writer is not only likely to sum up their life so far, but also to reveal to the reader a personal attitude or philosophy on how to live.

Autobiography language

● **Time connectives:** A skilful use of time connectives is essential for the writer to maintain the chronology of the text.

● **Verbs:** The author should expect to write in the past tense about previous events and achievements. However, there are likely to be occasions when other tenses are appropriate.

As the author is the subject of the text, the first person must be used.

Autobiography style

The style will reflect how the writer wants to be regarded by the reader, so the tone may be formal or informal. It is quite acceptable to use an informal tone in an autobiography.

Why you need to know these facts

● Biography and autobiography are two strains of the same genre. The texts may be similar, but there are important differences that the children will need to know. For example, as writers, confusion of third- and first-person writing would be a basic error.

● The children may not have noticed the use, by some writers, of a rhetorical question in a biography. Having this device at their fingertips will expand the children's writing skills.

● This is an opportunity to revise the difficult concept of the passive voice. Children need regular writing practice in its formation and use; they must know when it is appropriate; and they must be aware of its impersonal effect on their text.

● The children need to remember that their non-fiction writing does not always have to be formal in tone. An autobiography is both about and by the writer, and the tone chosen can help reveal the personality – informality may be appropriate.

Vocabulary

Autobiography – a life-story of an individual written by that person.
Biography – a life-story of an individual by another author.
Ghostwriter – a person who may be paid to do most of the writing in someone's autobiography.

Amazing facts

Famous, busy people may pay a ghostwriter to write some or most of the words of their autobiography for them.

Common misconceptions

A biography does not have to be about someone who is no longer alive. Many authors write biographies of living people.

Questions

Is writing a biography about a living person and a dead person the same? Many aspects are the same, for example: key events and people in the subject's life. However, when writing about a living person, the writer must be prepared for the subject's reaction to the text.

Handy tip

When writing a biography, check regularly that you have not lapsed into using *I…* A biography must be written in the third person.

Teaching ideas

● Ask the children to write a biography about an author. They should carry out research and write notes on key events and achievements in the author's life, planning their text before writing it.

● Ask everyone to choose a famous sporting hero. Suggest that the star wants to write an autobiography in time for the high-selling Christmas period but needs a ghostwriter. Allow time for research, note-making, and planning content and style, then use extended writing sessions for the children to write sample chapters of the autobiography.

● Ask the children to write their own autobiographies. Suggest that their readers will be other children in the school. The writers need to pick out key events and achievements from their lives so far, to select a tone that suits their personality and the impression they want to make on readers, and to consider their concluding paragraphs.

Writing additional information

Subject facts

In some information books, the writer supports the main text with additional sections. These should enable the reader to access the book's information more easily. Alphabetical order is often used for these sections to help the reader use them more quickly.

Contents
This comes at the front of the book. It should list the book's chapters in sequential order. The writer may include a subtitle for each chapter, informing the reader of what the chapter will cover.

Appendix
Some writers have non-essential, but useful, information to write after the main text. This could take the form of tables or more detailed information that may be referred to in the main sections of the book.

Glossary
The glossary comprises a list of the technical words and terms used in the text that are likely to be unfamiliar to the reader. Each term is written in bold font and alphabetical order;

beside each word a definition is provided. The glossary should be placed towards the end of the book, but before the index. Writers sometimes make it part of the appendix.

Index

This section is placed at the end of the book and provides a comprehensive list of the book's contents. The index should be sorted into key words, which are listed alphabetically, followed by the page number(s) where they are referred to, separated by commas.

Why you need to know these facts

● Understanding what the additional information sections are and how, when and where the writer should provide them will add to the children's writing competence.

● The children need to recognise the importance of layout, order and presentation in these texts. As writers, they need to remember that the reader is looking for specific information. By writing these sections correctly, they will put the audience on the correct reading pathway.

● Some of these texts may be outside the children's writing experience. They will need practise to acquire the succinct writing style needed in, for example, a website or a glossary.

Vocabulary

Alphabetical order – listed in the order in which the first letters of those words appear in the alphabet.
Appendix – a section that the writer adds to a document to provide non-essential or illustrative information.
Contents – a summary of the subject-matter of a book, usually in the form of a list of titles of chapters.
Glossary – a part of a text, sometimes included in the appendix, in which the writer defines terms used that are likely to be unfamiliar to the reader.

Index – an alphabetical list, usually placed at the end of the book, of names and subjects that the writer has mentioned in the book, and the page references.

Website – a collection of linked pages on the World Wide Web (www).

Amazing facts

The plural of 'appendix' is 'appendices'. Some tasks, such as compiling a dictionary, are likely to require numerous 'appendices'.

Common misconceptions

These sections are not unimportant extras! By writing these parts well, the non-fiction author can make the difference between creating a useful or confusing resource.

Teaching ideas

● Display randomly the words from a single age-appropriate dictionary, with the definitions hidden. Appoint the children as lexicographers to create the correct page. Remind them of features. Suggest creating a second version, this time for an illustrated dictionary for infants. Will they omit some words? Will they simplify definitions? Which definitions will need a picture as well as words?

● Provide the children with an index. Give them practice in using it by asking questions. Encourage scanning and awareness of alphabetical order to find page references. Ask the children to write four questions for a partner to answer using the index.

● Provide a piece of text with technical words that may be unfamiliar to the reader. Ask the children to make a glossary of them. Afterwards compare results, drawing attention to meanings that offer particular clarity.

● Agree on a broad subject for a topic, for example: habitats; our environment; the local area; animals and plants. Put the children into small groups to plan and then write a short information book. Ask them to share responsibility for writing the contents, index and glossary.

Resources

Non-fiction texts for inspiration:

Young Gardener by Stefan and Beverley Buczacki (Frances Lincoln Ltd)

The Concise Oxford Dictionary of Current English (Oxford University Press)

Managing My Life: My Autobiography by Alex Ferguson (Hodder and Stoughton)

Storyteller: The Life of Roald Dahl by Donald Sturrock (Harper Press)

Charles Dickens: A Life by Claire Tomalin (Penguin Viking)

Further reading:

Talk for Writing Across the Curriculum: How to Teach Non-Fiction Writing 5–12 years by Pie Corbett and Julia Strong (Open University Press)

Developing Literacy Non-Fiction Compendium by Christine Moorcroft and Ray Barker (A&C Black)

Improving Non-Fiction Writing by Alan Peat and Margaret McNeil (Nash Pollock Publishing)

Animals: Reading and Writing Non-Fiction: Teaching Guide (A&C Black)

Chapter 4

Poetry

Poets are very often put into a box of their own: unique, inspired and gifted, they must be made differently. Hence, we cannot attempt their form of writing. What misguided thinking! Poetry offers writing freedom to all of us. Punctuation rules can be waived; language can be played with; layout can be varied. Who could fail to enjoy this sort of writing?

So equip yourself with knowledge of poetry's technical terms, the names of its different forms and some of the language possibilities. You will teach more confidently and effectively, and you will inspire the children to write.

Before you write poetry

Subject facts

Although poetry writing offers infinite choice, most poets nevertheless follow certain conventions and the children will want to do the same. Familiarise them with ways in which poetry writing may differ from prose.

Lines
Poems are written in lines. The writer begins a new line when ready, not when the previous line is full. So the writer is free to vary line length.

Capital letters
The writer usually begins each line with a capital letter, even when they are not beginning a new sentence.

Punctuation

Poetry writers can decide what punctuation they want to use. For some, that means little punctuation; other writers follow the normal prose rules, but they begin every line with a capital letter.

Stanzas

A stanza or verse is a set of lines forming a section of a poem. A stanza lets the writer organise poetic writing in the way that a paragraph divides prose. Stanzas are usually four or more lines in length, with a clear break between them. The writer frequently follows a pattern throughout a poem.

Rhyme

Writers use the device of rhyme by making the final words in their lines end with identical sounds. (See pages 85–9.)

Vocabulary

The writer of poetry has the same vocabulary or word choices available as the prose writer. However, poetry allows the writer more language freedom. Words that in prose could be criticised as overblown, repetitive, exaggerated or archaic, in poetry become interesting and poetic.

Syntax

Syntax is how the writer puts words together. When writing poetry, it is acceptable to 'break' accepted syntax rules and to order words in an unusual way. For example: whereas a prose writer might write *He felt downhearted*; a poetry writer could write *Downhearted he felt*.

Figurative language

This is the use of metaphors or similes (see page 96). The writer's words are often less straightforward in poetry than in prose. Poetic descriptions may be more unusual, and comparisons (as in similes and metaphors) more frequent and often more subtle.

Rhythm

Rhythm is the beat of the poem. The poetry writer is more aware of this than the prose writer and often tries to maintain a steady beat in a poem, amending words and line length to suit it.

(See page 91 for more detail.)

Why you need to know these facts

● You may emphasise writing freedom, but most of us are conformists! At early stages, the children will want to write poems that look and read in the way they expect. They need to know the usual conventions that poetry writers follow.

● Writing poetry will not just happen! The children will need to play with words and lines. They will also want to think and talk. Having the correct vocabulary to talk about the number of *verses* they need, or the pairs of *rhyming* lines they are using will confirm to them that they are on the road to being a poetry writer.

● Almost as soon as the children start to write a poem, they will meet a writing quandary: *How long should my line be? Where do the full stops go? When should I use a capital letter? Do I leave any gaps?* Having this checklist of poetry facts, will give the children more writing confidence.

Vocabulary

Rhyme – the use of words ending in the same sound.
Rhythm – the beat of a poem.
Stanza – a set of lines in a poem (a 'verse').
Verse – an alternative word for stanza: a set of lines in a poem.

Common misconceptions

Stanzas do not have to be four lines in length. This length is merely a popular choice for many writers to work with.

Teaching ideas

● Ask the children to write a paragraph of prose (about six lines) describing the scene inside their classroom viewed through the eyes of a visitor. Then suggest changing the prose into eight to twelve lines of poetry. Encourage consideration of word deletions and changes, and word order, partner writers perhaps advising each other. Use the poems for a class display alongside the prose.

● Play a game in which you point out something nearby and the children write down what they can compare it to. Encourage unusual comparisons so that, when read aloud, listeners have to think for a moment about the connection. Give an example: stand a ruler on your table and say that it is like a sentry on duty. Can the children work out that the link is that they both stay straight? Keep the game fun and pressure-free with the writers working in pairs.

● Writing poetry requires a wide vocabulary. Expand the children's by supplying a list of adjectives: they must write one synonym and one antonym for each. Increase the number to two or more of each and challenge the children to write them in order of intensity. Encourage the children to become confident about using a thesaurus and a dictionary for more than spelling.

Making sound patterns

Subject facts

Rhyme

Rhyme is not an essential feature of poetry but it is a popular one. There are different types of rhyme, but all involve similarity between sounds.

● **Full rhyme or perfect rhyme:** This describes the final words in lines that end with identical vowel sounds. This is the one that the children will probably use readily in their writing.

*Up above the world so **high**,*
*Like a diamond in the **sky**!*

● **Half rhyme:** In half rhyme, words give the impression of rhyme but the rhyme is not perfect. Encourage the children to try using this sometimes. Here, only the final consonants match:

*Through the flap of the te**nt**,*
*There crawled a hungry a**nt**.*

● **Internal rhyme:** When a rhyme is created within a single line of poetry it is called an internal rhyme. This could be achieved at first by joining two of their rhyming lines together to make one. This will make them aware of greater writing possibilities. Edgar Allen Poe frequently uses internal rhyme as here in 'The Raven':

*Once upon a midnight **dreary**, while I pondered weak and **weary**,*
Over many a quaint and curious volume of forgotten lore-
*While I nodded, nearly **napping**, suddenly there came a **tapping**,*

● **Assonance:** The repetition of vowel sounds in words close to one another is often used by poets to establish mood or to emphasise a word's meaning. For example, Edgar Allen Poe uses assonance in 'The Bells': the happy mood of verse 2 talks of *mellow wedding bells* and *golden notes*; by verse 4 assonance helps to create a sombre mood:

In the silence of the night,
How we shiver with affright
At the menace of their tone.

● **Consonance:** Consonance is the repetition at close intervals of the final consonants of accented syllables in important words. For example, in Samuel Taylor Coleridge's 'Rime of the Ancient Mariner' the /st/ sound evokes a beating rhythm:

Higher and higher every day,
Till over the mast at noon—'
The Wedding-Guest here beat his breast,
For he heard the loud bassoon.

● **Eye rhyme:** Words that look the same but are actually pronounced differently is called 'eye rhyme', such as *bough* and *rough*. The opening of Shakespeare's Sonnet 18, is an example:

> *Shall I compare thee to a summer's day?*
> *Thou art more lovely and more temperate:*
> *Rough winds do shake the darling buds of May,*
> *And summer's lease hath all too short a date:*

Here, *temperate* and *date* look as though they rhyme, but natural pronunciation of *temperate* does not produce a rhyme with *date*.

Rhyming patterns

Rhyming patterns are created by the end words of the lines of a poem. Look at these nursery lines:

> *Twinkle, twinkle, little star,*
> *How I wonder what you are!*

In this pattern, rhyming lines are arranged in pairs, or couplets. In order to check the rhyming pattern, it is usual to label the end of the first line **A**. If the second line of the verse ends with a rhyme, the same letter is used; a new letter is used only when a line ends with a new sound. Hence, in this example, the full poem's rhyming pattern is seen to consist of rhyming couplets, and uses two final sounds (as indicated by two letters):

> *Twinkle, twinkle, little star,*   **A**
> *How I wonder what you are!*   **A**
> *Up above the words so high,*   **B**
> *Like a diamond in the sky!*   **B**
> *Twinkle, twinkle, little star,*   **A**
> *How I wonder what you are!*   **A**

Rhyming patterns vary considerably between poems. In 'Please Mrs Butler', Allan Ahlberg uses an ABCB pattern in each verse:

> *Keep it in your hand, dear.*   **A**
> *Hide it up your vest.*   **B**
> *Swallow it if you like, my love.*   **C**
> *Do what you think best.*   **B**

More common is the ABAB pattern in 'The Owl and the Pussy-cat' by Edward Lear:

> The Owl and the Pussy-cat went to sea   **A**
> In a beautiful pea-green boat,   **B**
> They took some honey, and plenty of money,   **A**
> Wrapped up in a five-pound note.   **B**

Clerihews

A clerihew is a short, humorous poem made up of two rhyming couplets. The lines can be of any length, but the first line must mention the name of the person who is the subject of the poem. Invented by Edmund Clerihew Bentley, this is an effective form for making a humorous comment about somebody. The inclusion of rhyme is likely to make the short verses memorable. John Foster writes about Dracula:

> Count Dracula
> At blood-sports is quite spectacular.
> He hunts for prey at dead of night
> And always gets in the first bite.

Why you need to know these facts

● When children start writing poetry, they usually try to make it rhyme. Rhyme is an enjoyable starting point and exploring it brings confidence in their mastery of language. They need to understand what 'rhyme' means, how they are formed and the types and patterns available.

● Sound is an essential part of poetry and the children should be encouraged to read aloud the rhyming lines they have written. It will become clear to them that rhyme results from sound; hence their phonological awareness will develop.

● As the children discover ways to look for and use effective rhymes in their writing, their vocabulary will widen. Searching for words with similarly ending sounds will bring an enrichment and enjoyment of language.

Vocabulary

Assonance – the repetition of vowel sounds in closely placed words.

Clerihew – a short, two-couplet, light-hearted verse about the person named in the first line.

Consonance – the repetition at close intervals of the final consonants of accented syllables in important words.

Couplet – two consecutive lines of poetry that function as a pair and usually rhyme.

Phoneme – a unit of sound in a word, represented by one, two, three or four letters.

Phonological – to do with sounds in language.

Amazing facts

However much you search, you will not find a rhyme for *month*: there is no rhyming word in the English language.

Questions

Does poetry have to rhyme?
Definitely not! Rhyme is a wonderful way to enhance poetry, but it is not essential. Certainly, forced rhymes which jar to the ear and add little to the poem's mood or meaning should be avoided.

Handy tip

When writing poetry, make regular pauses and read your lines aloud. You will hear what use you have made of rhyme, which sounds are effective and which can be improved.

Teaching ideas

● Recite pairs of poetry lines. Pause before the end of each couplet for the children to say the final word:

> Jack and Jill
> Went up the... hill.

> Little Jack Horner,
> Sat in a... corner.

> One, two, three, four, five,
> Once I caught a fish... alive.

Discuss why it was easy to provide the final words – the children may have known the rhymes by heart but the sounds of the final words also made them easy to work out.

● Recite this incomplete rhyme for the children to guess the missing word:

> Hush, quiet, don't say a word!
> Up there flies a little...

Is there agreement on *bird*? Can the children justify their decision? Introduce the word 'rhyme' and define it as *the use of words ending in the same sound*. Supply some opening lines, and ask the children to write a rhyming second line for each, so that their new nursery verses are fun and memorable for small children. Try these first lines:
- Now Cinderella could go to the ball,
- Then Goldilocks sat down in the chair,
- The Princess slept in a bed so high,
- Hansel and Gretel shivered with cold,
- Then Goldilocks tried the middle-sized bed,

● Write words on the whiteboard in red, ensuring many of them are monosyllabic (one syllable). For example: *calf; light; part; king; vein; keen; write; blow; friend; after; delay; apart; weight;*

repeat; world; course; purse; bigger. Can the children write rhyming partners? Write some in blue next to their partner words. Select one pair. Ask: *Can we compose lines ending in these words? Is there a linking subject?* Write a rhyming couplet together.

● Let the children, in pairs, compose a rhyming couplet from a pair of rhyming words. Groups of four could present their verses to one another or the class. Save the couplets for the next activity. Ask partners from the previous activity to re-read their rhyming couplet. Let them choose a new pair of words to write another rhyming couplet on a similar theme. Can they join both couplets into one verse? Will one couplet follow the other in an AABB rhyme sequence or slot into the other as ABAB? What title will they give their short poem? Can the other children, when the poem is read aloud, identify the rhyming pattern?

● List people from traditional stories or history. Write their names, adapting if necessary so that rhymes are possible. For example: *Robin Hood; Wizard Merlin/Merlin the Wizard; Elizabeth Fry; Florence Nightingale; Queen Elizabeth the First; King Henry the Eight; Neil Armstrong; Edmund Clerihew Bentley.* Emphasise the rhyming couplets and humour as the children write a clerihew, perhaps with a partner.

Playing with rhythm and language

Subject facts

Rhythm

Rhythm is the musical element of a poem. Also referred to as the poem's metre, it is similar to the beat in music. It is this mixture of stressed and unstressed syllables that determines the rhythm of a poem. Each pair of unstressed and stressed syllables makes a unit called a 'foot'. These feet involve a pattern of stresses responsible for the poetic metre. There are a number of possible metrical patterns, but four of them are popular when writing in English: 'iamb', 'trochee', 'anapaest' and 'dactyl'. This chart explains their variations:

Foot	Adjective	Stress pattern	Examples
iamb	iambic	da-**dum**	be**cause**; the **horse**
trochee	trochaic	**dum**da	**count**ing; **said** it
anapaest	anapaestic	da-da-**dum**	under**line**
dactyl	dactylic	**dum**-da-da	**look** at me; **hor**rible

The iambic foot, da-**dum** (an unstressed syllable followed by a stressed syllable) is particularly popular in English poetry.

Iambic pentameter

This is the metre pattern frequently found in classic English poetry. Each line contains five feet. The line must have ten syllables, five of them unstressed and five stressed. For example:

> *Shall I / com **pare** / thee to / a **sum** / mer's **day?**
> *Thou **art** / more **love** / ly **and** / more **tem** / per **ate***
> 'Sonnet 18' by William Shakespeare

The two lines are shown here broken into feet by / and with their stressed syllables in bold.

Stanzas

The way the poem is structured into stanzas can affect the rhythm. For example, by writing the same number of lines in each stanza, as in 'Bed in Summer' by Robert Louis Stevenson, the writer sustains a pattern in the rhythm of the stanzas:

> *In winter I get up at night*
> *And dress by yellow candle-light.*
> *In summer, quite the other way,*
> *I have to go to bed by day.*
>
> *I have to go to bed and see*
> *The birds still hopping on the tree,*
> *Or hear the grown-up people's feet*
> *Still going past me in the street.*

Other writers use the stanza to draw attention to rhythm changes and therefore the words in those 'different' lines. Edward Lear in 'The Owl and the Pussycat' moves from long lines to two, repeated short lines in a pattern at the end of each stanza:

With a ring at the end of his nose,
His nose,
His nose,
With a ring at the end of his nose.

Literary devices

Poets often use the following two literary devices. Although they are different from rhyme, the writer has to again think about sound.

● **Alliteration:** In alliteration, the writer repeats a consonant sound (phoneme) at the start of closely positioned words.

He watched and waited.
At last, his eyes fixed on a free 'phone.
Swiftly, he swooped.

● **Assonance:** The writer repeats vowel sounds in words that are quite close to one another. Edgar Allan Poe in 'The Raven' repeats an *ur* sound and so adds emphasis to those words:

And the silken sad uncertain of each purple curtain

Why you need to know these facts

● Rhythm is an exciting part of poetry. The children will hear a poem's beat as they read another writer's words aloud. Recognising that rhythm helps bring the poem to life; the children will be inspired to discover some of the ways that they can bring it to their own lines.

● The children should be encouraged to write creatively, hence, many will not need all these facts yet. Nevertheless, these rhythm and language tools should be added gradually to their writing toolboxes. Being aware of metrical and stanza patterns, will add to children's writing pleasure and skill.

● Knowing about other literary devices linked to sound will add to the children's writing tools and expand their creative choices. With this will come greater writing confidence and freedom. They will realise that rhyme is effective, but does not have to be forced; there are other ways to draw attention to their poem's sounds.

Vocabulary

Alliteration – adjacent or closely connected words beginning with the same consonant sound.
Literary device – a writing device used to achieve a particular effect, for example, mood or emphasis.
Pentameter – a line of poetry with five metrical feet.

Common misconceptions

People often think that alliteration needs the same initial consonant. In fact, alliterative words may have different initial letters but they must produce the same sound, for example, *wrong/runway*.

Questions

Do all poems have a consistent rhythm?
No, writers often change the beat of a poem. Other poems read very much like prose.

When writing poetry, work on understanding rhythm is best done a little bit at a time, perhaps experimenting with the beat in just one stanza. Worries about metre should not frustrate poetic creativity.

Teaching ideas

● Call an attendance register with a difference! Allocate everyone a number, then call the numbers for the children to answer with their name in an alliterative phrase, for example: *jumping Jack* or *sunny Sarah*. Extend the game to a classroom object, point to it and when a child's name is called they should say an alliterative phrase and then choose an object for the next person.

● Choose a poem with a clear rhythm, such as 'From a Railway Carriage' by Robert Louis Stevenson, and record yourself reciting it. Play it to the children and ask them to follow the rhythm and clap the poem's beat. Can they hear where the beat falls and which syllables are stressed? Write the results on the whiteboard, writing *da* for an unstressed syllable, *DUM* for a stressed one. Organise similar independent or partner investigation into different lines from the poem. Encourage the children to read their *da, DUM* results aloud to someone.

● Challenge the children to write new lines for a poem with a clear rhythm, such as 'From a Railway Carriage'. Where in the poem will writers place their lines? When the writer recites them, can the class clap the rhythm?

● Use Edward Lear's 'The Owl and the Pussycat' and its rhythm changes as inspiration (see page 88). Ask the children to write a poem about another unlikely animal pair. Ask for four stanzas, in which there are two alternating rhythm patterns.

Using imagery

Subject facts

Imagery is the element of the poem through which the writer tries to ignite the reader's senses. By effective use of vocabulary and figurative language, the writer can create a vivid image to appeal to the reader's senses. We think of *image* and *picture* as synonymous, but not all poetic images are visual. The writer may evoke other senses.

Figurative language

For figurative language, the writer uses a simile or metaphor to create a particular impression or mood.

● **Simile:** A simile is an unexpected comparison, where the writer compares a subject in one category to something else in a very different category. Nevertheless, the writer must know that there is a point at which the two items are alike. The writer's aim is to draw attention to this and create an image in the reader's mind. For example, in 'From a Railway Carriage', Stevenson compares the sights seen from the speeding train to drops of strong rain – they are both so numerous and move so fast that you cannot look at them properly.

> *All of the sights of the hill and plain*
> *Fly as thick as driving rain;*

A simile, as here, is usually formed by the word *as* or *like*.

● **Metaphor:** A metaphor is also an unusual comparison, but a stronger one. The writer achieves this by omitting *as* or *like*; instead, the writer states that the subject *is* something else. A metaphor is a forceful way of comparing two very different things. In contrast with a simile, a metaphor allows the writer to use fewer words, and it forces the reader to find the similarities, often independently.

In this sonnet by Shakespeare, *The eye of heaven* represents the *sun*:

Sometime too hot the eye of heaven shines,
And often is his gold complexion dimmed;
And every fair from fair sometime declines,
By chance, or nature's changing course untrimmed;

● **Personification:** Personification is a form of metaphor wherein the writer attributes human qualities to non-human things. This is achieved by using language normally applied to only human action, when referring to non-human things. In his poem 'To Sleep', Wordsworth talks to sleep as if to a person:

Without thee what is all the morning's wealth?
Come, blessed barrier between day and day,
Dear mother of fresh thought and joyous health!

Why you need to know these facts

● Imagery can make the difference between prosaic and poetic writing. Using figurative language will enable the children to transform everyday descriptions into inspiring pieces of verse.

● Metaphors are not always straightforward, so too often teachers view them as a difficult complication to creative writing. However, metaphors are well worth the effort. Taking the trouble now to teach the children how to construct and use them will nurture greater confidence in them as poetry writers.

● 'Simile' and 'metaphor' should become familiar terms. Nevertheless, their construction can be easily confused. Time spent on explaining and understanding the differences will equip the children to use both forms confidently.

● Writers need to understand that there can be too much of a good thing. The children should learn about the perils of mixed metaphors, understand why these are best avoided and recognise that, for imagery, less can be more.

- Personification is exciting! Attributing human behaviour to a non-human object will open up new possibilities to the images the children can convey. They will feel that they are bringing their writing to life.

Vocabulary

Figurative language – expressive language, often using a simile or metaphor, to create a particular impression or mood.

Imagery – the use of language to create a vivid sensory image, often visual.

Metaphor – writing that describes something as if it were something else. It is a forceful way of comparing two very different things because it says that one thing *is* the other.

Personification – a form of metaphor, in which language relating to human action is used to refer to non-human things.

Simile – a comparison of a subject to something very different, in order to create an image in the reader's mind. It usually uses the word *as* or *like*.

Amazing facts

The word 'metaphor' comes from the Greek word *metapherin*, meaning *to transfer*.

Common misconceptions

Many writers think that metaphors are too difficult for them to create. In fact, they can be very simple, and save words. For example, when a poet writes *The classroom is Henry's prison*, a metaphor is created. The reader gains an image of Henry looking and feeling trapped inside his classroom because he has to stay there. The writer does not have to explain the comparison.

Questions

Is it effective to use more than one metaphor at once?
Be careful about mixed metaphors; the use of two or more metaphors at the same time is best avoided. They confuse the reader by creating too many images that may conflict. One metaphor usually has more impact.

Handy tip

When you want to create a simile, use *like* or *as*; when you want to create a metaphor, use *is*, *are*, *was* or *were*.

Teaching ideas

● Revise what a simile is. Provide a subject and ask the children to link it in a comparison using *like* and *as*. Emphasise that effective similes compare a subject to something very different.

● Read aloud these line openers. Let the children compose the second half, always beginning with *as* or *like*. Remind them to be imaginative but to know what the feature of similarity is between the subject and the thing they are comparing it to:
  • *The noisy wind was…*
  • *The heavy rain was…*
  • *The car struggled on…*
  • *The fog on the motorway was….*
  • *Lights in the distance were flashing…*
  • *Jack's white face…*
Read each line opener again, this time inviting individual children to read aloud their comparison. Can the other children identify the common feature in the comparison? Do they find the simile and its image effective?

● Show the children the similes below. Explain that the writer wants to use fewer words and make the reader think. Ask the children to convert the similes into metaphors.
  - *The noisy wind was like a wolf howling.*
  - *The heavy rain was like loud raps on a door.*
  - *The small car struggled on like a clock ticking more slowly.*
  - *The fog on the motorway was like a deep bowl of thick soup.*
  - *Lights in the distance were flashing like eyes blinking.*
  - *Jack's mouth felt dry like a hot desert.*

● Ask the children to write a poem, using personification, to address the sun to ask for it to shine. They should request the sun for actions and behaviour normally reserved for humans, for example: *wave your hand* or *be in a good mood*. Encourage drafting and editing before they write their final poems.

● Read the first half of a sentence to the children. Can they think of something completely different, but with a feature in common? Working individually or with a partner, they must complete your sentences so that they are metaphors.
  - *The hurricane was...*
  - *The shaking buildings were...*
  - *The uprooted trees...*
  - *The broken windows...*
  - *The racing river was...*
  - *The helpless people were...*
Save the children's writing for the next activity.

● In groups of two or four, ask the children to read their metaphors to one another. Ask the listeners to talk about their response to the metaphor. Can they identify the common feature? What image does the metaphor create in their mind? What sense does the image appeal to? As a class, listen to one metaphor from each group. Ask the children to draw or write a description of the image created for them. Compare the results. Does a metaphor always have the same effect on people?

● Ask the children to write a short poem on a generic subject, for example, *weather*. They must use a metaphor. Hold a poetry-reading session, the children reading their work to a partner, group or the whole class. Compile a class poetry anthology.

Humour and nonsense

Subject facts

Humour and nonsense poetry does not need to make sense – the writer can enjoy merely combining words, lines and stanzas together into a poem. The writer expects his poem to make the reader laugh or at least smile. Spike Milligan's poems fit into this category as does Edward Lear's 'The Jumblies':

> *And all night long they sailed away;*
> *And when the sun went down,*
> *They whistled and warbled a moony song*
> *To the echoing sound of a coppery gong,*
> *In the shade of the mountains brown.*
> *"O Timballo! How happy we are,*
> *When we live in a Sieve and a crockery-jar,*
> *And all night long in the moonlight pale,*
> *We sail away with a pea-green sail,*
> *In the shade of the mountains brown!"*

Onomatopoeia
Onomatopoeia is a literary device whereby the writer uses words that echo the sound associated with their meaning. Lear's poem quoted above may make little sense, but the onomatopoeic *whistled and warbled* song are clearly heard by the reader. Similarly, in 'The Fly' Anthony Thwaite reproduces the sound of his subject in the first line:

> *The fly's sick **whining buzz***

Tongue twisters
To compose a tongue twister, the writer relies on alliteration. By using alliteration a lot, the writer makes the poem difficult to say quickly, as here:

> *She sells sea shells*
> *On the seashore.*

Why you need to know these facts

● A label such as 'nonsense poetry' will foster the children's enthusiasm and expand their creative thinking. They will be relieved to learn that their writing does not always have to be serious and that poetic words, lines and rhymes do not always have to make sense.

Vocabulary

Onomatopoeia – the use of words that echo sounds associated with their meanings.
Tongue twister – a poem or phrase that relies on alliteration, and hence is difficult to say quickly.

Amazing facts

Spike Milligan, a famous writer of nonsense poetry, said in an interview that his favourite words were some meaningless ones that his father used to use: *bazonika dowser!*

Teaching ideas

● Ask the children if they know any tongue twisters. Give them this one by Colin West to try:

Toboggan
To begin to toboggan, first buy a toboggan,
But don't buy too big a toboggan.
(A too big a toboggan is not a toboggan
To buy to begin to toboggan.)

Let the children practise saying it to a partner. After a few minutes, can they recite it quickly as a class? Analyse why it is difficult to say quickly. (The repetition of the initial /t/ sound.)

Emphasise that length and word rhyme are optional, but alliteration is necessary when writing tongue twisters.

● Agree on possible opening lines for a tongue twister, all relating to your class, school or you. For example:
 • Clever Class Four in the closest classroom…
 • Today's teacher talked about time travel…
 • Seaview School is situated by the sea…

Let the children, in pairs or small groups, write a clerihew choosing one of your opening lines or composing one of their own. Share and enjoy the finished poems.

● Read Spike Milligan's 'On the Ning Nang Nong' to the children. Talk about its lack of sense and its play with alliterative and onomatopoeic words. What animals would the children have in their fantasy land? (Elephant; rhinoceros; alligator; dinosaur; hyena; hippopotamus.) Let them write about the animals and their noises and movements in a nonsense poem.

● Ask the children to list their favourite/most disliked sounds. Can they apply an onomatopoeic word to each? Can they expand each sound and onomatopoeic word into a line? How will they order the lines to write a poem?

● Morning time is a noisy rush in everyone's house! Suggest writing a poem about it. Share ideas on typical sounds: alarm clock; raised voices; footsteps; spoons scraping on dishes; dog barking; baby crying; door banging; car's engine. Ask the children to write a poem about their morning sounds. Encourage onomatopoeia.

A story to tell...

Subject facts

Narrative poetry
In a narrative poem, the writer tells a story. Sound and beat are often important, as is the division into stanzas, which may be used to distinguish between parts of the narrative poem's plot. On the

other hand, there is often irregularity in this type of poem, and lines and verses may be of random lengths and styles.

Ballads

Ballads are a form of narrative poem that the writer often intends to be set to music and sung. They have strong associations with childhood, so the language tends to be simple. The writer should include a setting, character, and events with a climax. The stanzas traditionally consist of four lines, two of which are likely to rhyme, and a chorus is a common writing feature. For example, in 'The Ballad of Bold Sir Greville', Jane Bower repeats the final words of this stanza to end some of the other stanzas in the poem:

> Bold Sir Greville he spurred his steed
> Afar across the wide countrye
> And came at last to a high grey tower
> To seek the love of his fair ladye.

Free verse

The writer of a poem that tells a story sometimes prefers to be unconstrained by patterns of rhyme or rhythm: this is called free verse. Its advantage is that it allows the writer greater freedom. Lines and stanzas may vary in length, and rhyming and metrical patterns may be ignored. Consequently, it may be more difficult for the reader to understand how the writer wants the lines to be read and understood. For this reason, the writer must organise the lines to guide the reader. Endings and beginnings of lines, as well as punctuation, all become more important as, for example, in 'Career Opportunity: Knight Required' by Bernard Young:

> Are you courageous, honourable
> and chivalrous?
> Do you enjoy wearing metal suits
> And enjoy being called Sir?
> Then this could be the job for you.

Why you need to know these facts

● The writer needs to know about the closeness of the written, spoken and sung word. It emphasises the importance of the writer 'listening' to words and lines of poetry while writing them.

● New writers of poetry will gain confidence from a poetry category called 'free verse'. The very name is liberating. It allows the writer to put aside the potential worries of rhyme and rhythm and concentrate on telling a story set out in poetic lines and stanzas.

● The children are already well-practised speakers and storytellers. The term 'narrative poetry' will reassure them that writing in this poetic form is something that they can do well.

Vocabulary

Ballad – a form of narrative poem that can also be a song.
Free verse – a poem that does not have to follow any rhyme or rhythmic rules.
Narrative poem – a poem that tells a story.

Amazing facts

Ballads probably derive their name from the medieval French dances *dongs* or *ballares*.

Common misconceptions

People do not associate songs with poetry. In fact, they are closely connected. Many songs have begun as lines of poetry; only later have they been put to music.

Handy tip

As the writer, sometimes put yourself in the place of the reader. Ask yourself: *Does my poem tell a clear story?*

Teaching ideas

● Revise a simple childhood story, for example, 'Little Red Riding Hood'. Propose retelling the story in the form of a ballad. Work together on a possible opening stanza:

> *Long, long ago, in a little house,*
> *Lived a girl both kind and good.*
> *With happy smile and special cloak,*
> *Went Little Red Riding Hood.*

Point out the rhyme, traditional of the stanza pattern in ballads. Explain that a refrain or chorus can be effective and ask: *Which words would you repeat?* Suggest repeating the last line or part of it to end some stanzas. Emphasise the benefit of having rhymes ready. Ask the children to write a collection of rhymes and half rhymes, for *Hood*.

● Return to your ballad's opening stanza from the previous activity. Remind the children about their rhymes and half rhymes. Organise small groups to write their ballads. Afterwards let the groups perform their poems to one another.

● Choose famous characters from legend: Robin Hood; Saint George; King Arthur; Dick Turpin. Alternatively, use fables or stories from history. Suggest that the children plan a narrative poem for their chosen person, using a storyboard to make sure that they will have a chronological plot.

● Use the storyboards from the last activity for the children to write a narrative poem. Encourage them to think first about

the poetic style they want to achieve. What about line length?
What sound and beat do they want? Will the division into stanzas
match parts of the story's plot?

● Ask the children to write a paragraph of prose telling
the brief story of one of the main characters in a class novel.
Afterwards, change your mind! Ask them to rewrite it as
a free-verse poem. The poem must be in lines, but other aspects
are up to them. What do they discover? Does it sound like
poetry? How important is correct punctuation for the reader
to make sense of the poem? Does their free verse work well?
Encourage another attempt with a subject of their choice.

Writing to be heard

Subject facts

Performance poetry

All poems benefit from oral readings, but some poems are
written specifically to be spoken aloud, either by one voice or
a group. They are poems to be performed.

Chorus

When the writer repeats words, a line or a stanza at intervals
during the poem, a chorus is created. For example, in 'The Dragon
Who Ate Our School' Nick Toczek alternates storytelling
stanzas with a stanza repeating the same praise of the dragon.
The writer's style suggests a single narrating voice for the main
verses, and a group voice for the chorus:

The day the dragon came to call,
she ate the gate, the playground wall
and, slate by slate, the roof and all,
the staffroom, gym, and entrance hall,
and every classroom, big or small.

So....
She's undeniably great.

She's absolutely cool,
the dragon who ate
the dragon who ate
the dragon who ate our school.

Pupils panicked. Teachers ran.
She flew at them with wide wingspan.
She slew a few and then began
to chew through the lollipop man,
two parked cars and a transit van.

Wow....!
She's undeniably great.
She's absolutely cool,
the dragon who ate
the dragon who ate
the dragon who ate our school.

In some performance poetry the writer composes lines that resemble a conversation. The spaces, stanzas and line content make it clear who is speaking. In 'Louder!' by Roger Stevens, a teacher and pupil rehearse for a school concert. The choice of font and the words make it clear who is speaking and how loudly:

Louder, Andrew. You're not trying.
Pro – ject – your – voice.
Take a b i g b r e a t h and louder!

Welcome everybody to our school concert...

For goodness sake, Andrew. LOUDER! LOUDER!

**WELCOME EVERYBODY TO OUR
SCHOOL CONCERT!**

Now, Andrew, there's no need to be silly.

Rap

Rap is a specific type of performance poetry. The writer creates a fast pace, strong rhythm and repetition, and is aware of links with some modern music. Caribbean and Afro-Caribbean cultures may be evident in the vocabulary, dialect and spelling.

Why you need to know these facts

● These facts will involve the children in writing poetic forms probably unthought of. The forms are exciting and modern, and through them the children will realise that the words in their everyday vocabulary can be used in the poetry that they write.

● The children will learn that poetry covers a wider field than they first believed, knowledge of which can only have a positive effect on them as writers. The children will be inspired to write more creatively and to incorporate a new variety of devices, as they consider the appearance of their poem.

Vocabulary

Dialect – distinctive grammar and vocabulary of a language, usually linked to geographical area.
Performance poetry – poetry written specifically for oral presentation.
Rap – performance poetry with its roots in the Caribbean and Afro-Caribbean cultures. There is a fast pace, strong rhythm and repetition, and dialect is evident.

Common misconceptions

Some writers believe that they cannot include the local words or dialect of their area. In fact, writers are inspired by the spoken language around them. It is appropriate that some of it finds its way into their poetry.

Handy tip

After writing some of your performance poem, ask a partner to read it aloud. Is their oral interpretation what you wanted? If not, consider what changes you need to make.

Questions

Does a conversation poem have to involve two parties?
No, writers write poems for more than two voices, or, in the case of monologues, just one voice.

Teaching ideas

● Remind the children of 'The Dragon Who Ate Our School' by Nick Toczek. Suggest writing similar, light-hearted poems about an imaginary, momentous day at school or home. What will happen? What will their chorus be? How often will they repeat it? Can they imagine the poem performed? Perform the poems.

● Ask groups to write conversation poems to link with a cross-curricular topic. They should write lines for each side of the conversation – perhaps a single voice for one side, group voices for the other. Remind them that it is not a playscript, so line content or font changes must make it clear who is speaking. Invite groups to perform their poem for the rest of the class.

● Share ideas on the starting lines for a rap – perhaps of an imaginary classroom scene. For example:

> *Miss took a guitar to school one day*
> *She twanged a string and started to play.*

Encourage partner or small group collaboration as the children write raps to perform to one another.

● Set the scene: a conversation between a child who has eaten the missing chocolate cake overnight and an irate parent who baked it the evening before. Let the children write a conversation poem. How will they make it obvious who is speaking while still being subtle? How will words show mood, feelings and volume?

Following a structure

Haiku

A haiku has a total of 17 syllables. Japanese in origin, each poem has three lines, arranged in a five, seven, five structure of syllables. These poems are often illustrated and are usually about the seasons, summing up a moment of beauty. For example, in 'Springtime' by Mel Somers:

> *Sunlight broken clouds,*
> *Whispers of life bringing forth*
> *Intermittent blooms.*

Tanka

A tanka is another Japanese poem. Similar to the haiku in content, it follows the same syllable pattern, but has two additional lines of seven syllables. Jill Townsend uses this form in 'When Leaves Pile Up':

> *When leaves pile up*
> *and scatter through the garden,*
> *I start to worry.*
> *It is time for a bonfire*
> *to set ideas alight.*

Cinquains

A cinquain also conforms to a standard syllable pattern. The poem has a total of 22 syllables in five lines, arranged in a two, four, six, eight, two pattern. The last line often has special impact, as in Adelaide Crapsey's 'November Night':

> *Listen…*
> *With faint dry sound,*
> *Like steps of passing ghosts,*
> *The leaves, frost-crisp'd, break from the trees*
> *And fall.*

Acrostic poems

An acrostic has a key word or phrase, usually formed by the highlighted first letter in each line. Sometimes the key word is formed by initial letters running down the centre of the poem or even at the ends of lines. The key word is usually the subject of the poem. For example, in 'Crocodile' by Christine Potter:

Crocodile
Resting in the
Ooze, unaware of
Cruel calumnies,
Or rumours, that she eats her offspring
Dozing, waiting for her eggs to hatch
In the blazing sun. Soon it will be time to
Leave this place, lovingly opening
Enormous jaws to carry her babies to the water.

Lists

In a list poem, the writer sometimes repeats a line or phrase, as in Colin West's 'Socks':

Long socks, short socks,
Any-sort-of-sport socks,
Thick socks, thin socks,
And 'these-have-just-come-in' socks.

● **Kennings:** A kenning is a list of expressions about a single subject. Usually, the writer uses just two words for each item and, therefore, each line. For example, in 'Penguin' by Sue Cowling:

Seal-teaser
Fish-seizer
Ice-lander
Storm-stander
Egg-cuddler
Warmhuddler
Long-waiter –
Belly-skater!

Why you need to know these facts

● An acrostic is interesting, achievable and easily accessible. Highlighted initial letters make the form clear. Having chosen a subject and key word, the children will find the limitations of beginning lines with those letters manageable.

● Everyone makes lists and kennings are fun! The form can become a game, or brain exercise, in which the writer searches for different ways to say the same thing without using the usual name. It will encourage the children to reflect widely and creatively, as they search for new vocabulary and think beyond the obvious.

● Writers at all levels like to put a label to their work. Knowing the names of different poetry categories will inform the children of the options available to them and choose an appropriate form.

● Writing rules, such as keeping to a number of syllables, will help children to control their writing and make them aware of the rhythm of their lines.

Vocabulary

Acrostic – a poem in which the first letter of each line, when read downwards, forms a word or phrase. This key word is sometimes down the centre of the poem or at the end of the lines.

Cinquain – a poem with a total of 22 syllables in five lines: two, four, six, eight, two syllables.

Haiku – a Japanese poem of 17 syllables in three lines: five, seven, five.

Kenning – a list poem, often consisting of expressions about a single subject. Usually, the writer uses just two words for each item and, therefore, each line.

List poetry – in a list poem, the writer sometimes repeats a line or phrase.

Tanka – a Japanese poem that follows the same syllable pattern as the haiku, but with two additional lines of seven syllables.

Amazing facts

- Adelaide Crapsey followed her interest in rhythm and metre and experimented with the Japanese haiku and tanka poems. As a result, she invented a new poetry form: the cinquain.

- The kenning originated in Anglo-Saxon poetry, where things were frequently described without using their names. Hence, a sword might have been referred to as *battle friend*.

Common misconceptions

The haiku and tanka are often confused. Remember that a haiku's syllable pattern is 5, 7, 5; a tanka's syllable pattern is 5, 7, 5, 7, 7.

Questions

Is a haiku poem written in the same way in Japanese and English?
Writers follow the same rules, but a Japanese haiku is traditionally printed in a single vertical line, divided into three phases.

Handy tip

Read your lines aloud as you write. It will become easier to count syllables accurately.

Teaching ideas

● Choose a broad theme for an acrostic poem such as a season. Ask the children to make notes that describe things and feelings they associate with that time. Let them decide on their key word. Will it be the name of the theme? Will it be one of the dominant words from their notes? Do the initial letters give them adequate writing freedom? Will any prove too restrictive? Once the children are happy with their key word, ask them to draft their poem. In the final draft, the key word must stand out and a title given

● List some famous figures, occupations, buildings, objects, or weapons, associated with a history topic. Good examples include: Henry VIII; Queen Victoria; a lamplighter; a lance; a quill pen. Can the children, with a partner, think of a two-word description without using the common name? Share ideas before the children, individually or with a partner, write a kenning about their chosen subject. For synonyms, a thesaurus and partner discussion will help.

● Follow up the last activity with a game in which children read aloud their mystery history kenning. Can the rest of the class figure out who or what is the subject of the poem?

● Choose a day when the scene outside clearly reflects the time of year. Create a quiet atmosphere as the children study the view from a window. Ask them to capture the moment's weather, or nature, in a poem. A haiku, tanka or cinquain would be an appropriate form.

● Talk about the Japanese poetry forms that focus on a moment of beauty and decide on a subject, for example, a blue sky. Give everyone a piece of paper to fold and cut into six pieces. As a word or phrase comes to their mind, ask them to write it on a piece of paper, before putting that piece to one side. When they return afterwards to the pieces, can they expand any phrase into a line? Should they replace a word to create alliteration? Would an onomatopoeic word be effective? Should the words on two pieces of paper be linked? Let the children choose a poetic form, or their own variety of one, and write.

● Ask the children to write *good* and *bad* kennings about: parents, a teenager, or little brothers or sisters. One kenning should be complimentary; one should present the (imaginary) person unfavourably.

Creating a form

Subject facts

In some poems, the writer shows less concern with sound and language and more with the layout or line structure of the work. Form and appearance may take precedence, but they have a relationship with the subject of the poem. The following three poetry types are very similar and some poems may have elements of all three.

Shape poetry

A shape poem has a distinctive layout on the page. Writers use the shape of words, lines and poem to depict an aspect of their subject. This is very obvious in Tony Mitton's poem about an octopus, in which the lines look like arms:

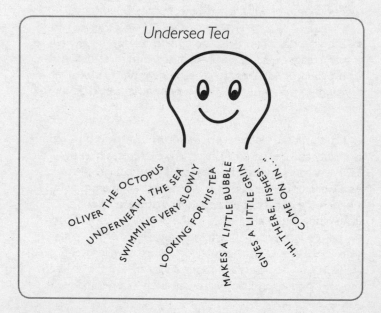

Undersea Tea

OLIVER THE OCTOPUS
UNDERNEATH THE SEA
SWIMMING VERY SLOWLY
LOOKING FOR HIS TEA
MAKES A LITTLE BUBBLE
GIVES A LITTLE GRIN
"HI THERE, FISHES!
COME ON IN"

Calligrams

In a calligram, the writer focuses on letter formation and font to represent aspects of the poem's subject. In 'Cats Can', Coral Rumble uses letters to draw a cat's arched back and to describe the blurred vision of near sleep:

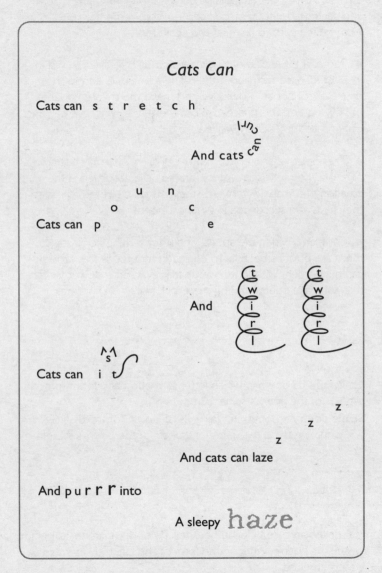

Cats Can

Cats can s t r e t c h

And cats can curl

Cats can p o u n c e

And twirl twirl

Cats can miss

And cats can laze z z z

And p u r r r into

A sleepy haze

Why you need to know these facts

● Children learn in different ways. Offering opportunities to put emphasis on a poem's appearance will broaden writing choice and particularly include those children for whom the visual element is a path to learning and achieving.

● Some of these poetry labels are unusual; the children will be interested in learning about them. The names will add to their data bank of poetic knowledge, and make the children aware of how other poets proceed. From there, they will have more options for their poetry writing.

● These poems are fun to create. Children who may not always perceive themselves as writers can become absorbed in the creation of a shape. Afterwards, they will be delighted to realise they have also succeeded in writing a poem.

● Calligrams widen the appeal of poetry writing. For instance, there are obvious benefits to using a computer, as the writer can experiment with font more readily. For some slower writers, this will make poetry writing more inclusive.

Vocabulary

Calligram – a poem in which letter formation and font represent aspects of the poem's subject.
Shape poetry – poetry in which visual layout (of words, lines and poem) reflects the shape of aspects of the poem's subject.

Amazing facts

A Frenchman called Guillaume Apollinaire was a famous calligram writer. His poem written in the form of the Eiffel Tower was greatly admired.

Common misconceptions

Shape poems do not have to be humorous. There are serious poems in this form. George Herbert's religious poem 'Easter Wings' is an example. Its text was originally printed with the text facing sideways to represent the wings of an angel.

Questions

Do these poetic forms have equal merit to other poems?
Yes, they require skill, inspiration, visual talent and word skills; they also bring a new emphasis on layout. As with all poems, the writer is using skill to affect the reader.

Handy tip

For shape poems and calligrams, write your words and then decide on the shapes to impose on the words, lines and letters. Make sure the results will be visible to the reader.

Teaching ideas

● Look again at Coral Rumble's calligram 'Cats Can': the deliberate misspelling and growing letters of *purrr* and the shaky font of *haze*. Point out *curl* and *stretch*. How do the children visualise the cat? Ask for sketches and compare results. What other actions are associated with cats? (Race; jump; tear; hunt; rip; prowl; leap; spit; scratch; wash; sleep.) How will the children make a word's letters evoke its meaning? Suggest using a computer to write their own *Cats can…* lines.

● Invite the children to create a display of shape poems that will have visitors rubbing their eyes in disbelief! Use the display title of 'Seeing spiders'. Their shape poem could have two parts – the drawn body of a spider, but eight lines of text to represent its legs. How will they set out each line on the page? (Sideways would work well.)

● Suggest the shape of a hexagon for the children to write concrete poetry. What things do they associate with a hexagon? (2D shapes; mathematics; honeycomb; bees; a snowflake.) Display hexagonal objects such as: a floor tile; a regular pencil; a nut (for a bolt); a glass holder for a candlestick. Ask the children to write interesting phrases about two or three hexagon associations.

● Follow up the previous activity, by giving the children a piece of paper and a hexagon to draw its outline firmly. On another piece of paper, placed over the first, they should write the text of their poem. Remind them to stay within their outline, and to keep to their subject (a hexagon) and their associations. Will they reveal one only in their last two lines? Encourage them to be ready to make changes to wording, line breaks and font size as dictated by the outline they can see. They will probably need to write a final, polished poem.

Resources

Poems from these books have been quoted in this chapter:

The Works by Paul Cookson (Macmillan Children's Books)
Classic Poems to Read Aloud Selected by James Berry (Kingfisher)
Please Mrs Butler by Allan Ahlberg (Puffin)
Classworks Literacy Year 5 by Eileen Jones (Nelson Thornes)
Classworks Fiction and Poetry Texts Year 4 by Eileen Jones (Nelson Thornes)
The Puffin Book of Utterly Brilliant Poetry Edited by Brian Patten (Puffin)
The Book of 1000 Poems Edited by J Murray Macbain (Collins Educational)
All of these anthologies will remind you of the variety of poetry and provide poems for the children to model their writing on.

Recommended anthologies:

The Works by Paul Cookson (Macmillan Children's Books) This is particularly useful. It has examples of even the unusual poetry forms, is divided clearly into sections, and provides accessible models for the children's own writing.

The Puffin Book of Utterly Brilliant Poetry Edited by Brian Patten (Puffin) This anthology is delightful. It will reassure the children that not all their writing has to be serious.

Classic Poems to Read Aloud Selected by James Berry (Kingfisher) The range covered here is wonderful. From Shakespeare to Roger McGough, James Berry selects poems to inspire and encourage the most reluctant writer.

The Book of 1000 Poems Edited by J Murray Macbain (Collins Educational) Every poem that you want to check on, or read to the children before they write, will be in here.

Further reading:

Teaching Children to Write Poetry by Sandy Brownjohn (Hodder Education)

How to Write: Poems by Wes Magee (QED Publishing)

Pizza, Pigs and Poetry: How to Write a Poem by Jack Prelutsky (Greenwillow Books)

How to Teach Poetry Writing by Michaela Morgan (Letts)

Jumpstart! Poetry: Games and Activities for Ages 7–12 by Pie Corbett (David Fulton Publishes)

Playscripts

When writing a playscript, the writer must keep in mind a different final form: the spoken word. The writer's text will lead to an oral play form, so they must provide the reader with both the words to be spoken, and advice on how to speak them.

Before writing a playscript

Subject facts

Of all forms of writing, the playscript conforms most strictly to a prescribed style and format. The reader can rightly expect the writer to adhere to these conventions. Before writing a playscript, the children must not only plan and prepare their storyline, but also become familiar with the writing style.

Planning and preparation
● **Genre:** The writer must decide in advance on the appropriate genre for the playscript and then follow additional writing conventions for that genre. (Each genre has a separate section in this chapter.)

● **Audience:** It is essential that the playwright considers not only the reader, but also the intended audience of the final oral play. This may affect the number, names and personalities of characters; the length and style of speeches written; the settings; and the scenes into which the writer divides the playscript.

● **Plot:** The first task is to plan the playscript's story, or 'plot'. The writer must be aware that the plot will be told through dialogue, while additional explanation and description will be provided through stage directions. The initial plan could look like this:

Title: *The Great Chocolate Money Mystery*

Scenes

1. Children buy chocolate discs; meet strange boy; boast how they will turn chocolate into money.

2. Children turn chocolate into 'money' with gold wrapping paper; same boy they met earlier delivers newspaper to their back door.

3. Children discover money is missing! A paw-print on floor.

4. Children shop while Dad talks to shopkeeper; on way home Dad tells them that shopkeeper thought it funny that a boy came in and tried to spend chocolate money!

5. Children pool information; suspect boy; Mum asks boy when he comes with paper; boy admits taking coins – wanted to buy present for his mother.

6. Boy comes with his mother and dog to return coins and apologise; full story comes out.

Structure

● **Cast:** The writer should begin the text with a list or 'cast' of characters. A brief explanation of who a character is and the relationship, if any, to other characters is also helpful to the reader.

● **Scenes and setting:** Scenes should be numbered and the settings identified. The scenes form the main part of the text and contain both stage directions and the characters' dialogue.

● **Stage directions:** Stage directions may be inserted at any point in the script. These are guiding comments and contain any additional information. This written advice should occur at the points at which it will present most benefit to the reader.

● **Characters' dialogue:** This is arguably the most important part of the text as it is what carries the story and what the final audience will hear.

Language
The writer must provide two kinds of text and the language used may vary accordingly:

● **Words for the reader's head:** In these words, the writer names characters; informs the reader of scene numbers and settings; and provides stage directions.

● **Words to say aloud:** These words form the main part of the writer's playscript and are the lines the characters must speak – the dialogue.

Presentation
Layout, font, letter case and punctuation will all help the reader to understand the text, and recognise what to read aloud and how. The usual conventions are:

● **Characters' names:** These are written on the left-hand side of the page, in bold and often followed by a colon.

● **Text for a character to speak:** Dialogue should be indented from the character name in a regular font (neither bold nor italic); no speech marks are to be used.

● **Stage directions:** Appear in italic, sometimes in brackets.

As writers, the children will find these font changes more manageable if they use a computer. Otherwise other conventions could be used, such as only using brackets for stage directions.

Why you need to know these facts

● Playscripts are different, interactive and often fun. As writers, the children will want to know how to create this experience for their readers.

● Playscripts involve their own technical vocabulary. Familiarity with and understanding of words such as 'scene', 'dialogue' and 'cast' will enable children to speak confidently about their writing.

● Success as playwrights depends partly on conforming to an established style. It is essential that the children learn about the presentational features of a playscript, understand their functions and practise using them.

● Playwrights fulfil a dual function in their writing: they provide the reader with both dialogue and stage directions. The second role is easily overlooked, but stage directions are an integral part of the written text. The children need to recognise this.

Vocabulary

Cast – list of characters (and their actors) in a play.
Character – an individual in a play.
Dialogue – written conversation to be spoken aloud by the play's characters.
Italics – faint, sloping writing that distinguishes itself from other text.
Playwright – a dramatist, the person who writes the play.
Scene – a portion of a play.
Stage directions – written instructions in the text of the play.

Teaching ideas

Keep the results of these activities for use in the Teaching ideas in other sections.

● Show the children a short clip from a television drama, preferably with few characters. As they watch it a few times, they should think about the place and character actions, and transcribe some of the dialogue in their exercise books. Can they imagine the clip as a playscript and write the script accordingly, using the standard conventions?

● Use a page containing mainly dialogue from a story. Put the children into groups that match the number of story characters and let them read the dialogue. Suggest that a playscript would make reading easier and the characters more lifelike. Ask the children to rewrite the page, using the format and conventions of a playscript.

● Look at the writer's initial plan for *The Great Chocolate Money Mystery* playscript (see Plot on pages 123–4). Alternatively, you can use plans that the children created during a previous activity. Discuss whether more detail in the plan would help the writer later. Suggest adding character names and helpful details, the setting (place and time) for each scene, and additional plot notes.

● Look again at the writer's initial plan for *The Great Chocolate Money Mystery* playscript (see Plot on pages 123–4). Point out that the final scene – Scene 7 – still needs planning. Encourage partner discussion. Should the ending be happy? Does it need a strong Christmas flavour? Can it link with the title? Ask the children to add the scene plan.

● Set the task of planning a playscript about a holiday mystery or adventure. Use partner discussion and plans from the previous activities. Ask questions to inspire ideas: *Will the play be a comedy or a tragedy (funny or sad)? Who will the characters be? Will there be main characters? What about the title and final line – will there be a link between them?*

Writing the dialogue

Subject facts

It is essential for a playwright to use appropriate vocabulary in the dialogue. This means taking into account the setting (time and place) and the character who will speak those words.
    There is a need when writing dialogue to think carefully about grammar and sentence construction and how the words will sound when eventually spoken. Spoken language breaks many of the conventions of written language and the children need to consider this

to ensure that the final script sounds natural. This is likely to include consideration of features such as contractions, accent and dialect.

The punctuation used in the dialogue can help the reader and speaker greatly. By choosing exclamation marks and question marks the writer can indicate a character's mood and tone of voice; with an ellipsis (…) there is a suggestion of a voice trailing off as thoughts or words are left incomplete, or an aside is spoken for only the audience to hear.

Why you need to know these facts

● The children may not have noticed that a playwright varies dialogue according to character, context, purpose, and formality of occasion. As playwrights, they must be ready to allow for these variations.

● The children will need to revise contractions – when and where to use an apostrophe. Natural speech usually joins some words together; if the children's written dialogue is to seem authentic, they must be aware of this.

● It is important for the children to consider their sentence construction. Writing dialogue demands that they keep 'listening' to what they have written: if the speech sounds too complicated for the character, they need to rewrite it.

● Punctuation is usually visible, but in dialogue, it also makes itself heard. By using punctuation such as exclamation marks or an unexpected question mark, the writer can guide the reader towards the appropriate tone for the speaking character.

Vocabulary

Contraction – shortened form of words that have been combined.
Syntax – sentence structure: how words are put together in a sentence.

Common misconceptions

New writers often think that writing dialogue must be easy! In fact, an experienced writer knows that revisions and rewriting may be needed to make speeches suit the characters.

Handy tip

When writing dialogue, keep pausing to read your words aloud to check that they sound appropriate for that character.

Teaching ideas

● Put the children into pairs to hold improvised informal conversations, but ban the use of contractions such as: *I've; where's; who's; can't; they've; you'd; won't; shan't; you're.* How many slips do the children make? Do they realise how unnatural their talk sounds?

● Ask the children to check the dialogue they have written in a recent story, perhaps reading some speeches aloud to a partner. Encourage self- and partner-assessment as they examine their dialogue for appropriate vocabulary, suitable syntax, formality and informality, and natural contractions. Let them pencil in changes that they now think are more appropriate.

● Provide a few lines of written dialogue between two characters. Include stage directions indicating how the characters speak and expressive punctuation in the dialogue. Use an ellipsis to suggest that more is to come. Explain that this is the end of Scene 1 of a writer's playscript. Organise pairs to discuss what may have been happening in this scene and to talk about the dialogue. How would they read it? What difference does the writer's choice of punctuation make?

● Build on the previous activity by asking them to work as a pair to write the scene's earlier dialogue. Encourage particular attention to meaningful punctuation that will help the speaker. Put pairs of children together to exchange playscripts. Are the writers pleased with the results when the new pair read the dialogue aloud? Did the reader gain the information they wanted to convey? Encourage helpful feedback as writers improve their dialogue so that punctuation and syntax achieve the results intended.

● Organise groups of three to agree on a one-scene play idea, perhaps linked to a forthcoming event. The playscript is needed urgently! Suggest writing the dialogue but omitting all punctuation. Ask the groups to exchange playscripts. How does the dialogue sound when the new group reads it aloud? Then let the children pass their scripts on to another group to read. Is the interpretation different again? Do the original writers realise how much punctuation matters to passing on the correct message to their reader?

● Ask the children to imagine planning characters for a play. Let them list the names of four characters they might use in the play. Suggest they add dialogue notes to the names: each character's style of sentences; typical vocabulary; likely contractions.

Presenting characters

Subject facts

The writer has three principal ways to provide the reader with basic information about the characters:

● **Cast list:** In the cast list, the writer names the character and states facts, usually relating the characters to one another, the plot or to their setting.

● **Stage directions:** The writer may include stage directions before, during or after a character's speech. These may refer to facial or body language, a tone of voice, an accent. All are ways in which the writer can present the reader with a clearer picture of the character being created.

● **Dialogue:** In the dialogue, the writer must assume the character's role and imagine how the words will sound when spoken aloud (as discussed in the previous section).

Adding character interest

The writer needs to create characters that are interesting in order to hold the reader's, and the eventual audience's, attention. The plan is a useful place for making additional notes that will help when writing the playscript. One useful question for the writer to keep in mind is: *What is it that will make this character interesting?* This main question may lead to subsequent questions. For example: *Does the character have a special power?* (A super power perhaps.) *Is their hobby out of the ordinary? Is their appearance funny?* (A haircut that they now regret.) *Do they have a peculiar mannerism? Do they favour a particular word? What surprising pet do they have?* The writer should jot down answers in the form of notes in additional boxes within the plan. These notes will help the writer to develop more complete characters.

Writing production notes

Production notes are written mainly for the play's producer. Although not essential, these notes may be supplied by the writer to give the reader further information. The writer may choose to write an introduction to the playscript, which is likely to take the form of production notes and include details of the characters and props. These details should be written with the intention of helping the reader to understand the characters further and to present them in a play. It can be an opportunity for the writer to provide supplementary character information that may be difficult to convey in the main playscript.

Why you need to know these facts

● The importance of planning the characters cannot be over-emphasised to the children. As novice writers, it would be easy for them to fall into the habit of creating one-dimensional characters to whom they have assigned little other than a name and superficial dialogue. Thoughtful planning will ensure that they have prepared enough ideas for their writing to give depth to their characters.

● Character creation is probably the playwright's most difficult task. The children need to be aware of the subtle character-writing opportunities presented by a playscript, and how to make effective use of them.

● The children may not have encountered a playscript for which the writer has written an introduction. They will appreciate the usefulness of character profiles in this section, as they recognise the writer's difficulty in demonstrating numerous aspects of a character in the other writing opportunities of a short playscript.

Vocabulary

Production notes – an introduction to a playscript, that may be supplied by the writer to give the reader further information.

Questions

Is there an ideal number of characters for a playscript?
The playscript can have any number of characters. Nevertheless, reader satisfaction and eventual oral performance are important considerations. Too many characters in a short playscript could result in 'cardboard' representations of characters

whose appearances are few and whose dialogue is brief.
The writer needs to allow sufficient appearances and dialogue
for characters to have depth and the audience to get to know
them. Furthermore, too many characters can complicate the
interactions between them, resulting in audience confusion
about who's who and why they are doing something.

Handy tip

Playwrights should aim to create characters that they can imagine
hearing and seeing. This is a good test of whether the reader will
succeed in bringing a character to life.

Teaching ideas

● Point out that sometimes playwrights and fiction writers
give their characters names or labels that hint at characteristics:
Horrid Henry, Mrs Wobble, Mr Bump and Mrs Twit are obvious
examples. Prepare a box of expressive first names or surnames.
Let the children pick out a name, extend the name if preferred,
and describe to a partner what this character might look like,
how they might behave and what they would enjoy doing.

● Display a cast list containing names, but no other details.
Ask the children to imagine what the characters are like and
make notes to use for character sketches. Remind them of the
purpose of these sketches – to give the reader an understanding
and mental picture of the characters. Suggest questions to ask
themselves: *What sort of voice does this character have? What style
of speech? How do they act and behave? How do they relate to
other characters?* Let the children write the sketches, using their
notes, but writing in sentences. Compare the results, discussing
the amount of variety in the children's interpretations of your
cast list.

● Play a game in which the children, spread around the room,
use posture to 'say' (without words) single-word exclamations

that you hold up. For example: *Come! Listen! Please! Leave!*
Leave these words on display and put the children into pairs to
choose and adopt the posture for one. From the actor's posture,
can their partner 'read' the word? Extend the activity to using
body language to suggest emotions: anger; disappointment;
apprehension; sadness.

● Provide the children with an extract from a playscript
but omit all the stage directions. Ask the children, in groups,
to add these to the playscript in order to help readers and
the audience understand the characters. When groups act out
their amended playscript, how much have they reinforced the
characters? Have they made them more interesting and lifelike
for the audience?

Writing for the stage or screen

Subject facts

In this genre, the writer's words are not only listened to but their
delivery is also watched. Character movements, gestures, facial
expressions and body language are all part of the playscript. The
writer must keep this visual element in mind to write a playscript
that will offer guidance to the reader, help deliver a successful
visual performance for the director, and provide a meaningful
experience for the audience. Screen productions offer more
distractions, visual and aural; the stage provides a smaller, more
focused setting, so more attention may need to be given to
writing the exact dialogue and stage directions.

Stage directions
● **Scenes:** Scene changes need to be planned carefully and at
appropriate places in the playscript. Will too many short scenes
interfere with the audience's concentration? How can a scene
change be made visually obvious?

● **Setting:** The scene can change by changing the setting.
The setting – time and place – should be stated at the beginning

of the scene. The writer must be aware of potential complications created by setting changes relating to scenery and props.

● **Characters:** Stage directions should be used to indicate which characters are in the scene at the beginning, if characters leave or enter the stage and who they are.

● **Face and body language:** The writer must remember that the speaker's facial expressions, body movements and gestures can give extra information, and this can be included as a stage direction.

Production notes

In addition to stage directions in the playscript, the playwright may use introductory production notes to offer the reader further information. This could include: a list of all the props you might need; any sound effects that may be required; suggested lighting, and so on.

Why you need to know these facts

● The children need to remember that the audience will see the speaker while hearing their words. Written speeches that seemed to read well on paper may repeat the obvious and, when spoken and watched, prove awkward and unnatural.

● As writers, the children will need to consider how they naturally behave as speakers. Do they repeat the name of the person they are looking at and talking to? Do they name people, places or things that they are pointing to? Do they always express their mood in words? They will realise that effective dialogue leaves some things unsaid: visible proximity, movements, gestures and facial expressions do much of the work.

● The importance of scene-planning should be emphasised – particularly their number and where to begin and end them. As writers, the children must appreciate the benefits of matching scene breaks with changes of setting. They will also need to consider the effects of the scene breaks on the audience.

- The children must view their stage directions as an integral part of the playscript. In this genre, the children may write with more precise detail, remembering that a speaker will be seen. Hence, the writer's directions may tell a speaker to move, gesture or adopt a facial expression.

Vocabulary

Props – accessories used to make a play realistic.
Scenery – the accessories used in theatre to make the stage resemble the supposed place of action.

Amazing facts

Filming problems sometimes mean changes to the script. When *Toy Story* was being made, the character Woody did not seem likeable enough. A team of writers had a week to rewrite the script so that the audience would like him!

Common misconceptions

The audience does not have to be told everything. When characters or objects can be seen by the audience, there are occasions when there is no need for the writer to use their names.

Handy tip

When writing a film script, keep putting yourself in the place of the producer and the audience. This will help you to keep your writing manageable, while still being rewarding to hear and watch.

Teaching ideas

● Introduce a stage-play character, for example: an innocent-looking, elderly lady to whom others pay little attention, yet who is a successful amateur detective. Ask the children to design her costume and label her props.

● Create a set of stage directions written on separate character cards. Divide the class into groups of about six. Give cards to one group at a time for the children to act as their card's named character and obey the stage directions. Challenge the rest of the class to recognise what actions they are portraying. Afterwards discuss the children's reaction to your stage directions: were they too vague or was there too much direction?

● Provide a short piece of written dialogue between two named characters. Make it obvious that their conversation or dispute is unfinished. Explain that their words end Scene 1 and ask the children to write Scene 2. Emphasise that the playscript will be used for stage or screen; this should affect their dialogue, stage directions and setting.

● Give the children the basic outline of a stage play: title; theme; primary characters; plot ideas. Put the children into groups of three, ask each child to write one of the play's scenes. When the scenes are put together, what sort of play results? Save the completed playscripts for later use.

● Use the finished playscripts and the same groups of three children from the previous activity. The groups print their play, join another group and compare plays. Which play would the six children prefer to perform? Give each group an opportunity to perform for the class. Invite audience comment, using a response sandwich: one favourable comment; one area for improvement; another favourable comment.

Writing for listening

Here, the playscript is listened to but the characters and setting are unseen. Radio plays and audio recordings provide the audience with sounds, voices and silence; the listener's mind has to do the rest. The writer's playscript must show an awareness of these factors.

Plot

In many ways, this playscript genre offers the writer the most freedom. There is an infinite choice of setting, as the demands of visual credibility no longer apply. Nevertheless, the listener's attention has to be held by a plot that can be followed, so, as playwrights, the children will be wise not to cram too many events or ideas into their scripts.

Structure

When writing for a listening audience, the writer has to keep setting the scene. This can be done by writing speeches for a narrator, using a monologue, writing helpful dialogue, or suggesting sound effects. In every scene or sequence, it is essential that the writer's words enable the listener to visualise correctly where characters are and what they are doing.

Characters

The writer must remember that the characters will not be seen, yet the audience must be able to distinguish one from another. Confusion can be avoided if the writer limits the number of characters, particularly in one conversation, and gives characters different styles of speaking.

Dialogue

The dialogue needs to feature speeches that differentiate characters by their vocabulary, speech mannerisms, and different tones of voice or accents. The listener will not see which characters are being addressed or what is being looked at, so the writer must use names – of people and things – more frequently than usual. The writer must remember that the listener will only know of a character's presence in a scene if that character speaks, or another character addresses him or her by name. Furthermore, the dialogue must inform the audience of changes: a new setting; the arrival or departure of a character. Use of the interior monologue may be required: in this type of speech, a single speaking character thinks aloud. Through this device, the writer may not only reveal a character's true, secret thoughts, but also create interesting contrasts, perhaps following a noisy sequence of multiple voices with a quiet speech of interior monologue.

Stage directions

● **Voice:** Instead of visual cues, the audience may have to infer information from the speaker's tone of voice or volume. Therefore the stage directions about the use of voice are very important.

● **Sound and silence:** This genre relies on sound. The writer uses stage directions to suggest noises such as a creaking door or atmospheric music. However, the writer may also suggest silence and pauses. These moments are an effective way to heighten suspense, or to convey worry or a peaceful atmosphere.

● **Sound effects:** Sound effects are noises that the play's producer has to manufacture artificially; the writer's task is to indicate what these sounds are. Sound effects bring credibility and atmosphere to scenes. Nevertheless, their purpose must be to help the listener to make sense of the action of the play, so the writer should keep their demand sparing and effective.

Why you need to know these facts

● The children will have to give more thought to the dialogue that they write and be reminded that the audience cannot see the speaking characters, only hear them. This will make the children alert for writing speeches that could confuse a listening audience. The added clarification of the name of the person being addressed will be one consideration.

● Silence is part of the listening experience. Realising this will make the children more aware of the audience's experience of playscripts, and encourage them to consider how meaningful pauses and moments of silence can inject atmosphere.

● The children may not have paid much previous attention to character differentiation, particularly in relation to voices. The difficulty now presented for the listener in identifying who is who will prompt the children to be innovative. They will enjoy thinking and writing creatively, and introducing speech mannerisms such as *um, er,* verbosity and flowery language.

Vocabulary

Interior monologue – a speech in which a character, alone, thinks aloud.
Monologue – when one character speaks alone.
Sound effects – sounds other than dialogue or music made artificially for use in a play.
Speech mannerism – a speech characteristic such as repetition, sounding pompous, *um* or *er.*

Amazing facts

The writers of radio drama cannot afford to bore the listeners. Radio producers have found that the ideal length of listening time is no more than 30 minutes. After that, the listener thinks of switching off.

Questions

Is this genre of playscript more difficult to write?
In many ways, the writer's task is easier and offers more freedom here. There are no limitations to settings or action. The writer can think and write originally because listeners will use their imaginations to picture the locations and happenings.

Teaching ideas

● Choose a group of children. Give them a playscript (unseen by the others) for a play that was written for stage or screen. After allowing time for rehearsal, ask them to perform the play behind a screen, as the others watch, facing the screen. Question the audience. Did they know what was happening and who was who? How difficult was it to follow the play?

● Put the children into groups of four, ask each to write two or three speeches for their group dialogue. Let the audience close their eyes when a group speaks the dialogue. Can they easily differentiate voices? Ask groups to make notes on distinctive speech mannerisms to give themselves before speaking their dialogue again. Is it easier for the audience now?

● Provide characters and an idea for the first scene of an adventure or mystery play. Put the children into small groups, matching the number of characters, to write the playscript for the scene. Encourage them to plan periods of silence in their production notes. Let unseen groups speak their scenes. Does silence intensify the suspense and drama?

● Set the scenario: three bored children have a wet day at the end of the summer holiday. What does their boredom lead them to discover? Could it be entry to a fantasy world? Ask partners to plan the plot of a playscript for a listening-only audience.

● Resume the previous activity. Encourage discussion as partners give names to their characters. Prompt consideration: *Will any characters have speech mannerisms? How many scenes will there be? Where are the settings? How will the listeners know when locations change? What is the title?* Let children expand their plans.

● Return to the plans from the previous activity. Ask the partners to write their playscript. Encourage them to read speeches aloud to each other, consider whether additional words are needed for a listening audience, and amend as necessary. Remind them to consider stage directions.

● Use the finished playscripts from the previous activity. Form larger groups of four or six, so that children can read their scenes to a new listening audience. Encourage the writers to use the listeners' feedback to make final changes. Supply recording equipment for the group members to help one another make an audio recording of each playscript. (Partners will need other group members so that they have enough voices for their characters.)

● Hold some play-listening sessions in which the listening audience make a fair assessment of their audience experience. They could fill in a review chart like this one:

Group	Highlight	How to improve

Afterwards ask the children to use their notes to write a review of no more than 200 words of one of the plays they listened to for a drama magazine.

Adapting stories

Subject facts

This is a popular form of playscript, both with writers and readers. For writers, the task may appear easy – the story is already there! However a playscript demands a very different structure and the writer must choose a story carefully for the adaptation to be successful.

Plot

The plot of the new playscript is already in place in the novel or short story that the writer is working from. Nevertheless, the playwright cannot just transfer one text into another structure. It is essential to choose a suitable story – one with a clear main plot and storyline. Decisions need to be made at the initial planning stage. How much of the story should be used?

Will it be the whole story or only sections? For example, AA Milne, in his play *Toad of Toad Hall*, extracts just Mr Toad's story from Kenneth Grahame's novel *The Wind in the Willows*.

Structure

The novelist has already provided a structure in the form of chapters, and this can help the playwright to plan the play. Chapter breaks often coincide with changes in the plot's setting. The play's scenes should also match changes in location or time so it may be possible to write scenes to match chapters.

Omissions and changes

Even when adapting a complete story, the playwright has to omit and abbreviate some passages. Some chapters may be mainly descriptive and can be overlooked by the playwright or incorporated into other scenes. The novelist has time and space for long passages of description and detail; the playwright does not. Therefore the key aspects of a book need to be considered – will the story make sense if something is omitted? Will something else have to be changed? For example, in *Charlie and the Chocolate Factory: A Play*, Richard George omits lengthy descriptions and examples of the Bucket family's impoverished diet contained in Dahl's book, but still keeps the essential information of their reliance on cabbage soup.

Characters

The playwright must aim for authenticity in an adaptation and the characters are an integral part of the author's story. The main story characters must become the main characters in the playscript. Only very minor characters, with little bearing on the story's main plot, or perhaps merely presented as part of the writer's descriptive passages, should the playwright consider omitting.

Dialogue

The storywriter's dialogue is a bonus to the playwright as it is ready to use. By using it, the playwright ensures that the adaptation retains the tone, message and style of the original text. How the story dialogue is spoken must also be maintained in the stage directions for the actor. However, the story's speeches may prove too long or too numerous, so the playwright must be prepared to make appropriate cuts. In addition, there are the passages, pages and even chapters of description to consider. Their plot message may be necessary to the playscript, so the writer may convert them into dialogue, spoken by the characters, or into explanatory 'bridge' speeches for a narrator.

Stage directions

Stage directions are likely to be of great importance in this playscript genre. The playwright – without the storywriter's descriptive leisure – has to present the same character. The playwright needs to give information on voice, settings and body and facial language. All of these should fill the gaps left by omissions from the story text.

Why you need to know these facts

● Adaptation of a short story or a section of a story into a different form appeals to children. For many, writing this genre of playscript seems more manageable because a plot and characters are already in place. With the additional guidance of these facts, the children will write more confidently and competently.

● It is important to point out the association between chapters and scenes. The children will find it helpful to know that, although there does not have to be a precise match, the original story's chapters can help them to make decisions about scenes.

● Struggling to include all the storywriter's detail is a common mistake. By giving them practice in identifying a story plot's main events, the children will recognise that their playscript needs to focus on those.

● Dialogue is the core of every playscript. In this genre, there is the added task of writing speeches that suit the lines taken from the author's original story. Recognising this will make the children more aware of using words to create subtle differences in tone.

● The children may not have used the character of a narrator before. They will benefit from learning that through the words they write for their narrator, they can abbreviate sections of the original story and bridge scenes.

Vocabulary

Adaptation – a text that is derived from a pre-existing plot and rewritten to suit a different medium.
Narrator – a person who remains outside the play's plot and who describes events between the speeches of the other characters.

Amazing facts

Some playscripts can become as popular as the original stories behind them. Michael Morpurgo's popular novel, *War Horse* has been highly praised. Its playscript adaptation by Nick Stafford and Steven Spielberg's film adaptation have garnered just as much acclaim.

Common misconceptions

The adaptation does not have to cover the whole story or have the same name.

Handy tip

Draw a diagram, mapping out the original story's plot. Fill in characters, settings and scenes. This will help you to identify what you want to include or omit in your adaptation.

Teaching ideas

● Use a short story or a considerable section of a class novel, selecting a section with plenty of action. Ask the children to make a diagram, identifying the main events, before adding characters and settings. Will the chapter breaks help them to decide on scene breaks? How many settings are there? Let the children note their conclusion and keep them for the next activity.

● Return to the previous activity. Let the children check the novelist's writing for dialogue. How much of these words will the children use? Encourage them to write, edit and revise, then to consider their finished playscript dialogue critically. Have they retained the character's tone and voice in their writing?

● Give the children practice in writing in the same voice as a novelist. Look at a playscript that was adapted from a story, such as *Toad of Toad Hall*, and discuss how the characters are presented: Toad – impulsive, outspoken and full of excuses; the Judge – strict, easily shocked and formal; the Policeman – pompous, self-important and easily offended. Read half a scene aloud with the class and then ask the children to write the rest of the scene. When they listen to one another's writing, does the dialogue suit the original lines?

● Story description may need to be reduced when adapted into a plays. Use part of a novel that you are reading, for example, Chapter 1 of *The Railway Children* by E Nesbit. There is considerable detail and action in the chapter, not all of it necessary in a playscript. Challenge the children to decide how much detail and how much of Nesbit's dialogue to include when they write their playscript.

● Suggest planning and writing a playscript (of about four scenes) for younger children using a fairy tale. Emphasise the need for a comprehensive plan: plot; scenes; settings; characters. Point out the dual restrictions on the dialogue: it must suit the character speaking it, and its syntax and vocabulary must be age-appropriate.

● Return to the previous task. The children need to reduce their number of scenes to two or three. How can they do this while still covering the whole fairy tale? Ask them to introduce a narrator. They will need to consider: when the narrator will speak; the content of the narrator's speeches; the tone and style of the language. Remind them that a narrator can bridge story gaps and add missing detail to the playscript.

Resources

These books have been quoted in this chapter:

Charlie and the Chocolate Factory: A Play Adapted by Richard George (Puffin Books)
The BFG: Plays for Children Adapted by David Wood (Puffin Books)
Toad of Toad Hall by AA Milne (Samuel French Ltd)
Troll Towers by Eileen Jones (Scholastic Ltd)
Saved in time by Eileen Jones (Scholastic Ltd)
Hold the Front Page! by Eileen Jones (Scholastic Ltd)
The Great Chocolate Money Mystery by Eileen Jones (Scholastic Ltd)
The Witches: Plays for Children Adapted by David Wood (Puffin Books)

Further reading:

Creative Activities for Plot, Character and Setting by Teresa Grainger, Andrew Lambirth, Kathy Goouch and Garry Walton (Scholastic Ltd)
The Art and Craft of Playwriting by Jeffrey Hatcher (Story Press)
So You Want to be a Playwright? by Tim Fountain (Nick Hern Books)
Pupils as Playwrights: Drama, Literacy and Playwriting by Brian Woolland (Trentham Books)
Teaching Primary Drama by Brian Woolland (Longman)

Chapter 6

Media

Media writing can take many forms. The range extends from factual texts and information notices, to personal opinion and exaggerated claims. The writing may be linked to newspapers and magazines, radio and television formal notices (for example, advice about what to do during a pandemic), advertisements, or electronic messages, such as email or text messages. Inevitably, style and tone varies, and this must be evident in the language, tone and sometimes the appearance of the writer's finished text.

Before writing a media text

Subject facts

Planning and preparation
● **Subject:** The writer's first task is to consider the subject. This may dictate the most appropriate form and context for the writing.

● **Research:** In most media writing, there is at least an element of truth. Some forms allow for greater amounts of personal opinion than others but the writer is likely to need a background of factual information. Books, other media texts, product leaflets, the internet, first-hand knowledge and interviews of other people are all possible sources of information.

● **Note-making:** As with other non-fiction texts, research information should be presented in note-form. For more information see page 49–51.

● **Genre:** The writer must decide on the correct genre of media writing, and follow the conventions for that genre. (Each genre has a dedicated section in this chapter.)

● **Pictorial plans:** Pictures can be a helpful addition when writing an advertisement. At this planning stage, the writer may make rough sketches of the pictures to be included, and note the proposed location of words on the page.

Why you need to know these facts

● All writing benefits from planning, but with media texts it is particularly important. The writer's subject and intention must be decided; the genre chosen; research done; notes written; and a plan made. It is essential that the children realise that this preparatory work precedes writing the text.

● The writer will need to consider more carefully than usual the context of the proposed text. Language, tone, style and format are all related to the media genre used. Understanding the distinctions between genres and knowing their related writing conventions and styles are essential facts for the media writer when preparing.

● Some media texts offer the writer an opportunity to express personal opinions. Writing a letter to a newspaper or submitting a personal article to a magazine is a real-life experience that the children may be offered. Knowing the correct way to write will give them the confidence to act on the opportunity.

● Electronic writing is part of the modern world. The children are likely to perceive it as more relevant to their lives than many traditional writing forms. They will be eager to identify the different electronic message forms and to understand the writing styles and conventions involved.

Vocabulary

Email – electronic mail that is written and sent to a recipient across the internet or other computer networks.
Media – the means of communication, usually a newspaper, magazine, television, radio or the internet.

Handy tip

Remember that planning notes are for personal use later. Make sure that the writing style, layout, organisational devices and abbreviations will also suit you as a reader.

Teaching ideas

● These activities will often result in notes or a plan. Keep them for use in the Teaching ideas in later sections.

● Use partner discussion to talk about note-making. Can the partners list important features of notes? Compare results as a class and agree on a list to make and keep.

● Set the scenario: the children have been asked by the editor of a travel magazine to write an article about a local town or tourist attraction. Suggest that they first plan the content of their article. Books and websites will help them to carry out research and check facts. Emphasise the need for accurate recording of names as they make notes to keep for a later section.

● Appoint the children as editors planning to run a newspaper campaign on a topical issue. Ideas could include: extending the school day; changing the summer holiday. Suggest that the editors prepare by making notes for and against the chosen subject. Emphasise clarity so that they will be able to work from their notes in a later session.

Writing articles and reports

Subject facts

Articles and reports are both written for newspapers and magazines. However, the journalist has a different focus in the two types of text: in articles, the focus is interest; in reports, the focus is news.

Articles

- **Context:** The writer or journalist may write an article for a newspaper or a magazine.

- **Content:** An article should contain some facts. There is plenty of scope for the writer's opinion, but the inclusion of facts demonstrates knowledge of the chosen topic.

Structure

- **Headline:** The journalist needs to create a headline with wording and appearance to catch the reader's attention and interest. Font is much larger than in the main body text and probably bold. Phrasing is short, snappy and not necessarily a complete sentence.

- **Subheading:** A subheading, also known as a standfirst, is often used to clarify the basic statement of the headline prior to the article text.

- **Byline:** Authorship of the text should be claimed under the headline.

- **Introduction:** A broad, introductory sentence that indicates what the article is about is an effective start for the writer.

- **Headings and subheadings:** These organisational devices, in addition to paragraphs, are useful tools. They allow the article writer to divide the text into sections and are an efficient way to hold the reader's interest and aid comprehension.

Language

● **Powerful verbs and informative adverbs:** These are important features for the writer to use. Powerful verbs keep the text stimulating and vivid; informative adverbs supply detail.

● **Person:** When writing an article, there is ample scope to express a personal opinion. Consequently, the writer may move frequently between using the third and first person.

Layout

The writer should be aware that columns are part of the conventional layout of newspaper and magazine articles. In addition, it is useful to separate paragraphs or sections of the text with headings and subheadings.

Pictorial element

When relevant, the writer may choose to include pictures – diagrams, illustrations or photographs – with explanatory captions as needed. All these are effective tools as the writer seeks to add appeal to the article, and therefore interest the reader.

Reports

● **Context:** The writer or journalist may write a report for a newspaper or a magazine, but newspapers are the more common context. Newspaper report writing involves a degree of urgency. The writer is likely to be under a time pressure, so the children will need practice in having time restrictions as they write short reports. They need to be aware that leading with the topic sentence and then moving on to detail will help newspaper readers who are also usually short of time.

● **Content:** The writer's aim must be to convey news: therefore, the text is factual. Nevertheless, newspaper space is usually limited and the writer wants the reader to be interested as well as informed, so details are selected with care. Quotations from people involved in the events being reported may add realism.

Structure

● **Headline:** The journalist must create a headline to grab the reader's attention and encourage further reading.

- **Standfirst:** The writer may add detail to the headline's information with a standfirst. The standfirst is a subheading located below the headline in a font distinct from the body of the report. It clarifies the headline prior to the report text.

- **Byline:** The byline gives the name, and often the position, of the writer of the report. Bylines are traditionally placed between the headline and the text of the report.

- **Introduction:** The journalist should use the first sentence as a topic sentence, explaining what the report will be about.

- **Paragraphs:** It is advisable to write in short paragraphs. These enable the reader to follow the facts and locate information more easily and quickly.

- **Ending:** An effective finish is essential in order for the writer to hold the reader's attention to the end.

Language
- **Person:** The writer usually writes in the third person.

Layout
Columns are part of the conventional layout of newspaper and magazine reports. This can place limitations on the amount of text that will fit in the available space.

Pictorial element
Reports are about reality. By including a relevant photograph, the writer may enhance this reality and add interest and authenticity. Explanatory captions should be used as needed.

Why you need to know these facts

- Articles and reports have the same media context and a similar appearance. Hence, their labels are sometimes carelessly juxtaposed. However, there is a difference between the two texts and it is essential that the children understand this distinction, and the writing implications involved.

● Newspaper and magazine text layout is very different from that of a book. In the media forms, there is an emphasis on columns and a more precise use of space. The children need to realise that space cannot be used casually and so this writing type brings the additional task of meeting a word-count requirement, in order to match the column inches available. The children will need practice in selecting appropriate detail to inform and interest the reader.

● It is important to consider the use of pictures in articles and reports within the space available. They must be proportionate to the length of their text, its topic, and the additional interest or information offered to the reader.

● Young children often confuse first- and third-person writing. It is important to distinguish between them, consider their uses in this genre, and revise the respective personal and possessive pronouns.

Vocabulary

Article – a text written to be of interest to a newspaper or magazine reader.
Byline – a line at the top of a newspaper or magazine article or report carrying the writer's name.
Caption – the explanatory wording attached to a picture.
Headline – the title, usually written in large or bold font.
Standfirst – a short sentence that fills out some detail of the story.

Amazing facts

A newspaper writer has to be very careful about facts. If something untrue is written that could ruin someone's reputation, it is an offence called 'libel'. The newspaper could be sued for this.

Common misconceptions

'Report' and 'article' are not synonymous: an article is written for the purpose of interest; a report is written to convey news.

Questions

Are writers' articles and reports ever changed?
Yes! Media writers have to get used to the copy editor cutting some of their writing because it is long-winded or is taking up too much space.

Handy tip

Remember that newspaper and magazine editors are usually short of space. So write clearly without wasting words, keep to the point and avoid repetition.

Teaching ideas

● Use partner discussion for the children to talk about writing articles and reports. Can the partners make lists of their respective writing features? Compare results as a class and agree on lists for the children to make and keep as reference sheets.

● Show the children some short reports in a newspaper. Point out their brevity, and suggest that this is because of their minor importance. Talk about recent school or area events that might fall into this category; that is, worthy of a report in the school newspaper but not serious enough to warrant much space. Ask the children to write a report of one of these events.

● Following an article-planning activity, ask the children to consider page layout and column space for their article. What headings will they use? Would one or two pictures make the article more interesting and informative for the reader? Is there enough space to fit it all in? Ask the children to draft the layout in their exercise books or on a separate piece of paper.

● Involve the children in exciting and realistic drama. For example: collect them from the playground after break, warning them that there has been an incident! Show a disturbed classroom with items taken and a message left. Issue the children with notebooks and pencils. As reporters, they should note facts and evidence, interview the teacher and classroom assistants, collect quotes and take pictures. Suggest that the local newspaper will clear its front page for the report; hence, the writers have ample space. Let the children work individually or in pairs.

● Explain that many national newspapers include a weekly column by a journalist who writes about their current life. The writer's aim is to keep readers interested, and often amused, with personal and family news about incidents often similar to the readers' lives. Set the children the task of writing their own weekly article. What interesting name will they give it? How will they keep readers entertained enough to want to read next week's article? Encourage them to write about funny situations.

Writing a newspaper editorial

Subject facts

An editorial is the section of a newspaper that expresses a clear viewpoint. In it, the writer acts as the newspaper's voice and expresses a clear viewpoint on a current issue. The first inside page is a traditional place, but many newspapers favour a later page.

Structure
● **Headline:** The writer needs to use a headline, and often a subheading, that will catch the reader's attention. Large, bold font; phrases; pithy wording; and alliteration may all contribute.

- **Opening:** The main text needs to begin with an introduction of the issue. The writer achieves this with a clear opening statement or question.

- **Arguments:** It is essential that the arguments are clear and logical. In order to make them powerful, it is advisable for the writer to support them with reasons, evidence, statistics or quotes from people. Generally, the writer should use at least three arguments in an editorial because research has shown that this number is needed to persuade the reader.

- **Evidence:** The editorial viewpoint must seem logical. The evidence of supporting facts should provide proof that the editorial stance on an issue is sound.

- **Statistics:** Numbers bolster words, adding weight to the editorial viewpoint. However, they must always be checked and their sources quoted.

- **Reasons:** Reasons add to the impression that this viewpoint is the logical one for the reader to adopt. A reason may be effectively written in the form of a question. For example: *If cars cause so many accidents, then why do we not advocate more cycling?*

- **Quotes:** Quotes from authoritative voices, concerned people and experts in this field add credibility to the editorial. It is essential that the quotes are correct.

- **Conclusion:** The writer should finish with a summary of the arguments and a final appeal to the reader with a definite opinion on the issue.

Style

There is a need to consider the type of newspaper involved and its usual style of writing. The writer must be aware of the readership of the newspaper and adopt a tone to suit that audience.

Language

- **Logical connectives:** By using logical connectives (*obviously; this proves that; as a result; consequently; so; of course; meaning that; because; therefore*, and so on), the writer makes the editorial's arguments and viewpoint seem the obviously correct ones. Hence the reader is likely to be persuaded.

● **Verbs:** The writing is generally in the present tense.

● **Emotive vocabulary:** The writer's choice of words can be critical to the reader's support. Powerful and emotive words can create strong feelings and persuade the reader that the writer's view is correct.

● **Layout/pictorial element:** The layout should be clear and straightforward. Pictures are unlikely to feature, but a bold headline with engaging punctuation – often an exclamation mark or question mark – paragraphs, font differentiation between headings and the body of the text, all contribute to a readable text.

Why you need to know these facts

● Newspaper writing should become part of the children's writing repertoire. Some children may have little familiarity with newspapers and they will need help in identifying the different sections.

● The editorial, although relatively short, may be viewed as a newspaper's most influential section. The children need to realise that when writing the editorial they are expressing a viewpoint on behalf of the newspaper as a whole and so they must write in the newspaper's tone and style.

● It is essential that, as writers, the children are reminded of the power of the words that they use. In the choice of their arguments and the words they select to express them, editorial writers have the ability to persuade readers to agree with their viewpoints. The children need to be aware of this.

● Logical connectives are useful language tools. In an editorial, a writer can make effective use of them to strengthen arguments. This is an opportunity for the children to extend their bank of logical connectives and to practise their use.

Vocabulary

Editorial – newspaper piece written by or under the responsibility of the editor.
Logical connective – a linking word or phrase that deals with cause and effect.

Common misconceptions

The editorial does not have to be written by the editor. Nevertheless, it is the direct responsibility of the editor.

Handy tip

Write a headline that will grab the reader's attention. There is more chance that the reader will go on to read the rest of the text.

Teaching ideas

- Return to the notes that the children made during the fourth Teaching ideas activity in the first section of this chapter (Before writing a media text on page 150). Explain that their newspaper has decided to publish an editorial on the issue and the children have to write it. Emphasise the need, even though they refer to both sides of the issue, to have a clear opinion and to select arguments and language to persuade the reader to that viewpoint. Ask for a formal style, suitable for a newspaper such as *The Times* or *The Telegraph*.

- Talk about a current issue from newspapers or television news. List points from both sides of the issue. Progress to partner discussion, as children decide on their viewpoint for an editorial, and gather their arguments and supporting evidence, statistics or quotes. What will their attention-grabbing headline be? What will they write as a subheading?

● Provide the children with a selection of two or three headlines for which they must write an editorial. Group the children depending on which headline they chose and ask them to compare the results.

● Read out two editorials from real newspapers – perhaps one local and the other national. Ask the children to discuss the paper's readership and to comment on the differences in style and tone of the editorials.

● Ask the children to choose one of a selection of newspapers and write an editorial in a similar style. Partners may work separately on writing different parts of the editorial before they combine the text. Read the finished pieces to the class and ask if they can work out which newspaper it is for.

● Remind the children of the editorial read to them for the last activity. Read out the editorial from a newspaper aimed at a different readership, preferably on the same subject. How is the tone different? Is it more or less emotive? Are sentences longer or shorter? Which editorial is more formal? Ask the children to use the editorial written for their last activity. Working with partners or individually, they must adapt it to the new newspaper. Some arguments and supporting factors may change as well as language and sentences.

Writing advertisements

Subject facts

An advertisement may feature in a newspaper or magazine, on television or radio, or on a website. Its purpose is to sell a product or attract customers. Its inclusion in all these media forms must be paid for; therefore, the writer wants to create a text that will be noticed by the target audience. That means that the text must be written with that intended audience in mind.

Text structure

● **Sentence structure:** The writer should construct sentences that suit the topic. A serious advertisement for a charity is likely to contain short, conventional sentences and end them with full stops, question marks or exclamation marks. In a frivolous advertisement for a chocolate bar, the writer may use phrases:

> *Packed with taste and health*
> *A luscious creamy centre*
> *A healthy layer of nuts*
> *Perfect!*

● **Questions:** The advertisement writer will find that questions are a useful device: they can be addressed directly to the reader, and so draw the reader in. For example, this newspaper advertisement for the town's new gymnasium begins with a question:

> *Would YOU like an easy way to get fit?*

The writer has used *you* to create a personal relationship with the reader. The wording of the question will probably lead to a silent, affirmative answer; and the reader will continue.

● **Exclamations:** Exclamation marks provide the writer with ready-made impact: their dramatic form demand attentions. The writer may use them in short sentences or after single words. All draw the reader's eye to the language and messages involved.

> *Free trial! No payment up front! Pay and exercise!*

● **Dashes:** A dash is a useful punctuation mark in informal advertisements. The writer may sometimes use it instead of the more formal full stop. For example:

> *Try the taste now – you won't regret it!*

Language

● **Persuasive words:** Persuasion often depends on involving the reader. In the opening line quoted earlier – *Would YOU like an easy way to get fit?* – the writer immediately starts to persuade the reader by using *you* to form an alliance with them, and offering empathy and sympathy with *easy*.

● **Adjectives:** The writer's choice of adjectives is very important. Exaggerated words are acceptable as it is important to create an impression that will sway the reader's opinion. For example, in an advertisement quoted earlier, *luscious, creamy* and *healthy* satisfy the reader's wish to buy chocolate that is delicious, yet not unhealthy.

● **Superlatives:** Superlatives are the extreme form of an adjective, and the advertisement writer is likely to make frequent use of them. *Best, finest* and *most sensible* all allow the writer to create an impression that the reader will find difficult to ignore:

> *Do you want the best fitness programme for you?*
> *Visit the finest gym in town.*
> *It will be the most sensible decision you've ever made!*

● **Alliteration:** Light-hearted subjects allow the writer to play with words, using puns or linguistic devices. For example, alliteration makes phrases memorable in this advertisement for goods in a shop's summer sale:

> *FABULOUS FASHION!   HOLIDAY HOLD-ALLS!   BEACH BOOKS!*

● **Assonance:** Assonance is another linguistic device that uses sound. Again the writer can make the advertisement's words and messages memorable to the reader or listener. For example, the gym may have:

> *great rates; clean machines*

● **Rhyme:** A catchy rhyme is an effective way for the writer to make sure that the subject's name is remembered. The writer is likely to use a memorable rhyming jingle for television and radio advertisements as well as for printed media forms. For example:

> *Time for a snack?*
> *Time for a NIK-NAK!*

Presentation

- **Placing:** The writer must consider the positioning of text. What will the reader notice first? When could the reader become bored? The writer may place text in an unexpected place in the advertisement or at an unusual orientation to make the reader notice and read on.

- **Boxes and shapes:** The use of boxes and shapes allow the writer to be creative with the layout and keep the reader alert. Text boxes and the *curly cloud* in the examples below are other layout devices available to the writer:

- **Speech bubbles:** By using speech bubbles in the advertisement, the writer can add variety to the form of the text. In addition, if the spoken words are attributed to an authoritative source, they add support to the claims made in the advertisement.

- **Symbols:** The writer must be aware that the readers of media advertisements may have little time to spare. Ticks, crosses and mathematical symbols all provide the writer with quick, interesting methods of communication. Here the writer sums up easily and appealingly the benefits of the gym:

  YOU + OUR GYM = FITNESS SORTED!

- **Lettering:** The style and size of lettering are further tools at the writer's disposal. Making the most favourable word (such as *free*) large and upper case will draw a reader's attention to it.

● **Illustrations:** Illustrations are an integral part of many printed advertisements. The writer may use a combination of diagrams and text to ensure easy, quick understanding by the reader. The pictures are worthwhile as they probably communicate more effectively with the busy reader than words could do.

Why you need to know these facts

● More than many texts, advertisements encourage the writer to be creative. They offer opportunities to combine illustration and text, and they encourage awareness of both the sound and the appearance of words. The children will benefit greatly from access to these exciting writing opportunities.

● This is an ideal opportunity to revise and practise linguistic devices such as alliteration and assonance. They will expand the children's vocabulary and make them aware of how their words will sound and how they will affect the reader or listener.

● These facts continually emphasise persuasion. The children need to be reminded of their potential power as writers. Their words, if used thoughtfully, can persuade the reader. However, they also need to understand that, with advertisements, the writer has to struggle to ensure that the words are read.

● Puns and rhymes are fun, and the children will enjoy experimenting with them. Realising that the puns and rhymes can also be purposeful will add to their knowledge and experience as writers.

Vocabulary

Pun – a play on the meaning of words.

Amazing facts

A whole page of a newspaper or magazine may be taken up by just one advertisement! A large company such as Marks and Spencer sometimes pays to advertise a special promotion – for example, its new range of winter clothing – on a number of pages.

Common misconceptions

Newspaper advertisements do not have to form any links with the newspaper's articles and reports. They are quite separate pieces of text.

Questions

Do writers always work independently on the whole advertisement? No, many writers prefer just to write the text and offer only suggestions for illustrations. The actual pictures are then done by someone else.

Teaching ideas

● Set the task: to think of a new food product for children's lunch boxes, to appeal to both children and their parents. Share ideas as a class before paired discussion. Ask them to write three phrases with impact for a magazine advertisement for the food, each phrase using different alliteration. Can they add a name for the food? Suggest writing separate phrases about different aspects, such as: taste, varieties, ingredients, health value and cost. Are the children going to use text boxes or bullet points?

● The children must write an advertisement for their company's breakfast cereal. Quotations from people already using and who are pleased with the product would help to persuade the reader. Let the children decide on two or three characters to use (for example, a health-conscious mother; a father concerned about cost; a fussy child; a celebrity) and work out the wording for their speech bubbles.

● Remind the children of the benefits of writing a catchy slogan, preferably with rhyme. Emphasise that the slogan needs to be short for the reader to find it memorable – and that it should contain the name of the product (a game or toy). Encourage partners to share ideas, experiment with phrases and say words aloud before they write their slogan.

● Display a familiar school product: an interactive whiteboard; a printer; a computer; an electric pencil sharpener; a school meal tray; PE equipment. Propose that the school is selling it and needs to advertise it in local and school magazines. Ask the children to make notes on interesting features, how to give the advertisement impact, a drawing or photograph to use, and the amount and location of the text before they write the advertisement.

● Collect samples of printed advertisements and cut them up into sections: headlines; quotations; pictures; slogans and so on. In pairs, ask the children to use the pieces to create an advertisement for a new product that a teacher might like. The children can present these to you, or create a display board of the printed advertisements.

Writing to the media

Subject facts

For the writer, the media can present a difficult and unknown audience. It involves a fast world where attention spans may be short. The writer has to adapt by offering visual clarity and fast access.

Context

This writing may have many contexts, for example, a letter to a newspaper, or communication with a radio or television

company. Even a relatively formal text, such as a letter to
a newspaper, is frequently transmitted by modern electronic
means. Newspapers usually contain details of how and where
to make written contact with them.

Content

In a letter to a newspaper or magazine, the writer is often
commenting on something printed in a previous issue or
a current news topic. When communicating with a radio or
television company, the writer may have a number of reasons: to
comment on a programme; to request information; to complain
or praise; to suggest new ideas; to share in an online discussion.
Electronic communication is encouraged by television and
radio companies, and often becomes part of the live debate
of a discussion programme, for example: the writer may be
watching a discussion programme, send an opinion via an email
or a social media website, and it is read out as the programme
is still being transmitted. In these 'instant' messages, writers may
write in phrases or use common abbreviations.

Style

● **Brevity:** In all these forms of text, the writer is competing
for the reader's attention, and cannot afford to waste space
or words. Emails are likely to be read quickly and displayed
on-screen; some social-media websites limit the writer's
message to 140 characters.

● **Appropriate:** The text's purpose helps to dictate the style.
If writing a letter to be printed in a newspaper or magazine,
the writer should conform to the style used in the publication;
and that is often relatively formal. 'Letters to the Editor' pages in
newspapers, for example, *The Times*, demonstrate that Standard
English, correctly constructed sentences, and a name and address
are essential.

However, such letters could be written and posted, be part
of an email or be written as separate computer documents and
attached to an email. In a short email or other electronic message
to an on-air television discussion programme, such as *Question
Time*, the writer's words may have an informal immediacy evident
with incomplete sentences or popular abbreviations. For example:

Layout

When a communication has to be more detailed, for example, sending a proposal for a new television programme, the writer must consider its layout carefully.

● **Bullet points:** Bullet points allow attention to be drawn to important points and the statements to be clearly separated. For example, a writer emails a television producer with an idea for a play. The email is short, but in clear polite English with an informative subject line. The writer includes a play summary that will be quick to read. Bullet points increase the clarity.

● **Spacing:** Spacing is important if communication is going to be dealt with quickly. The writer is wise, when typing on a computer keyboard, to select 1.5 or double line spacing, to make reading the text more comfortable. Similarly, in an email, the writer should avoid too many solid blocks of text. Two or three short paragraphs are preferable, with an empty line between them.

Why you need to know these facts

● With this writing, the children will need to have greater awareness of the reader's time pressures. The disciplines of writing concisely and presenting text clearly and helpfully are useful skills that need to be practised.

• Many of the references in this section concern very modern forms of communication. The children's experiences will vary, and many will need help in understanding these new terms.

• It is important to recognise that the speed of electronic messages brings difficulties as well as benefits to the writer. This speed and ease of sending means that the recipient has more mail, so the writer has to consider how to get their message read and absorbed.

• Emails are probably already part of many older children's social lives. However, it is important that they understand that this informality is not always appropriate. A formal style will become increasingly suitable as they use emails in more serious contexts. This is an opportunity for them to learn and practise the skills of composing subject lines, writing concisely, expressing requests politely, and editing and proofreading before sending.

Vocabulary

Subject line – the place at the head of an email where the writer can type what the email is about.

Amazing facts

Anyone writing a letter to *The New York Times* has one chance in 21 of having the letter published. Letter writers to *The Washington Post* do much better: one in every eight letters is printed!

Common misconceptions

It is not always appealing to clutter the signature block of an email with witty quotations or drawings. They may irritate the reader. The appropriate contact information of name, address and phone number are what is needed.

When writing to a newspaper or magazine, remember the acronym **KISS**: **k**eep **i**t **s**hort and **s**imple. There is more chance of the letter or message being published.

Teaching ideas

● Find an appropriate child-friendly website forum or review site (many online retailers have the function to leave reviews and comments for other users which can then be further commented on by others). Explain that it is a discussion area, where users may post comments about the topic. Open some comments and replies and discuss them. Ask the children to write their own posts.

● Ask the children to think about a television or radio programme that they watch or listen to; let partners discuss aspects such as its length, style, format or storyline. Can they think of improvements that the producer could make – perhaps in its future plot, guests, format or presenters? Their proposal to the television or radio producer should be set out clearly and concisely. Suggest that their computer document should not exceed one side of A4 when printed.

● Point out that a media producer will be used to regularly receiving and inevitably discarding new ideas. An accompanying email must be sent with any proposal. Discuss important features: polite; concise language; main points to whet the reader's appetite and ensure that the attachment will be opened; a subject line that will mean something to the reader. Ask the children to write the email, attaching the document containing an idea for the magazine or television or radio programme.

● Show the children a long-established national newspaper with a formal style – for example, *The Times* or *The Telegraph*. Point out the length of an average letter. Explain the tradition of readers writing letters to the paper, commenting on current affairs, issues of the time, or points of interest. Printed letter writers are often important or famous, so ordinary people feel pleased to have their letters published. Ask the children to plan and write a letter that they hope will be published in a newspaper with a formal style. Encourage them to make the subject matter one of national interest or debate, for example: London's new statue or tallest landmark; the logo for a sports event; a change to the National Health Service. Encourage the children to edit their letters to keep within the average word count. Put them into groups to collaborate on a 'Letters to the Editor' page or let them enter their work on class pages to print and display.

Writing and alternative media presentation

Subject facts

Media text forms have not remained static since the 1990s. Now not every newspaper is read in its paper form; some are online. Books and magazines are also available in electronic form as well as paper. These modern changes may have implications for the writer as well as the reader.

Online newspapers

An online newspaper allows the reader to read on screen. It may be an online-only newspaper, or most frequently, it has a hardcopy connection. For example, *The Guardian* appears in both forms. Online newspapers may have RSS feeds (Really Simple Syndication) that are web pages, designed to be read by computers. The feeds provide the reader with constant updates of breaking news as it unfolds. Similarly, live blogs on the online newspaper's website, used in combination with social-media websites, ensure that the reader is kept up to date with news information and opinion.

● **Writing implications:** In online newspapers, the writer has a greater need to report news quickly and succinctly. The reader is likely to be in a hurry and demand news that is timely; hence the online writer must change a report as events change. The reader is likely to scan, rather than to read in detail, so short sentences, lively writing and immediate information are advisable. Pictures may be used where helpful.

● **Blogs:** Internet newspapers often have a news web-log site to which they invite writers to contribute messages and comments in the form of blogs. Examples of the blogs, written by readers of the newspaper, can be seen at www.guardian.co.uk/news/blog

Online magazines

As with newspapers, online magazines may be independent entities or have links with hardcopy magazines. For example, the educational magazine *Primary Teacher Update* is produced by MA Education in both forms. The articles and reports in the hardcopy version are available in the alternative online form.

● **Writing implications:** In many magazines, there are no changes between hardcopy and online versions. The writer's articles are reproduced with the same words in both forms; it is only the reading experience that changes.

● **Online resources:** In many hardcopy magazines, the writer can now make reference to additional written material available in the online version. The writer needs to produce these text document files for placing within the related online magazine, or to be accessed through hyperlinks from it.

● **Interactive material:** Interactive material is a reader expectation with some online magazines. In the case of a magazine for children and their teachers, the writer may provide interactive activities that can be reached via a link in the internet magazine.

Ebooks

This is another on-screen text that should be discussed at this point. The writer is unlikely to make writing adjustments, but the ebook's use and popularity are reminders of the demands that readers make for practicality, ease of reading and convenience. They are factors for the writer to keep in mind.

Why you need to know these facts

● Many of these media forms are new and the vocabulary related to them is expanding and evolving. Teachers need to stay up-to-date in this knowledge to pass on accurate information.

● Media changes are rapid. Many hardcopy magazines have disappeared in recent years. Writers need to realise that writing opportunities for the magazine may still exist, but they are now online.

● Readers' needs and demands exert considerable control over the forms and content of media writing. A reader's demand for instant access to timely news is important: it places pressure on the writer to amend reports and to produce new text quickly.

● The online resources linked to many online magazines make additional demands of the writer. There is a need to understand how to create interactive resources, video and audio files, and to incorporate them, or their links, into a written document.

Vocabulary

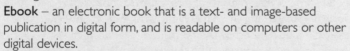

Blog – formed from the term 'web-log', a blog can be the online writing of an individual or of a number of writers.
Ebook – an electronic book that is a text- and image-based publication in digital form, and is readable on computers or other digital devices.
Interactive material – an electronic resource or game that allows interaction with the user.
Online magazine – a magazine that is published electronically, usually on the World Wide Web or internet.
Online newspaper – a newspaper that exists on the World Wide Web or internet, either separately or as an online version of a printed newspaper.
Online resources – word documents and other files available to the reader through the internet.

Amazing facts

By 2012, most newspapers had an online section. The demands of their readers made this essential!

Common misconceptions

Not all online newspapers have a paper version. For example, *The Southport Reporter*, introduced in the UK in 2000, is an independent web-only newspaper.

Questions

Is online reading usually free?
Newspapers and magazines vary. Some allow free access, but many retain access for most of their material to be read by subscribers only.

Handy tip

Read some online material regularly, for example a blog site, so that you are familiar with current changes and how electronic material is being used by the media.

Teaching ideas

● Introduce the children to the blog site for *The Guardian* newspaper at www.guardian.co.uk/news/blog Discuss some current news topics familiar to the children and ask them to write a report on one that would be suitable for this news blog. Create your own site where the children may enter their reports.

- Look at www.guardian.co.uk/news/blog again and investigate some of the comments after news reports (checking them first yourself for suitability). Comment on their length, wording and structure. Return to your own site from the previous task. Ask the children to read some news reports written by other children and to add comments to them.

- Visit Scholastic's online magazine for teaching children at KS1 and KS2. Point out the reference to Roald Dahl Day. Suggest that the children create an electronic resource for primary children, either about Roald Dahl or another popular author. The resource could consist of a worksheet that the teacher would be able to print and photocopy for the children's use.

- Return to the educational resources website used above. Look at some of the free interactive resources, for example, search with 'Start with the senses'. Investigate its use. Let the children add their own new text to each page. Can partners design a variation of the site to extend the children's learning?

- Talk about pressure for online news reports to stay up-to-date. Present a scenario: a flash flood or other emergency has occurred in the town; areas are blocked off; people have to evacuate from their homes; emergency accommodation has been provided. Ask the children to write the news report, but limit the time available to them. Mimic an RSS feed by providing a news feed on the whiteboard that they update every 5-10 minutes. This could be similar to "Breaking News" on TV at the bottom of the screen. Do the children need to amend their original report?

Resources

These publications or internet sites have been referred to in this chapter:

Child Education PLUS magazine (Scholastic Ltd)
The Times newspaper
The Times Letter page
The Daily Telegraph Twitter column
www.scholastic.co.uk
www.guardian.co.uk/news
www.guardian.co.uk/news/blog

Further reading:

Language and the Internet by David Crystal (Cambridge University Press)
Visual Approaches to Teaching Writing: Multimodal Literacy 5–11 by Eve Bearne and Helen Wolstencroft (Published in association with the UKLA)
Writing for the Internet: A Beginner's Guide to Writing Online by Lisa Mason (Kindle edition)

Glossary

Acrostic – a poem in which the first letter of each line, when read downwards, forms a word or phrase. This key word is sometimes down the centre of the poem or at the end of the lines.

Adaptation – a text that is derived from a pre-existing plot and rewritten to suit a different medium.

Adverb – a word that gives extra meaning to a verb. It may inform the reader *how, where, when* or *how often*.

Adverbial phrase – a group of words that functions in the same way as an adverb.

Alliteration – adjacent or closely connected words beginning with the same consonant sound.

Alphabetical order – listed in the order in which the first letters of those words appear in the alphabet.

Appendix – a section that the writer adds to a document to provide non-essential or illustrative information.

Article – a text written to be of interest to a newspaper or magazine reader.

Assonance – the repetition of vowel sounds in closely placed words.

Autobiography – a life-story of an individual written by that person.

Balance – a weighing of arguments.

Ballad – a form of narrative poem that can also be a song.

Biography – a life-story of an individual by another author.

Blog – formed from the term 'web-log', a blog can be the online writing of an individual or of a number of writers.

Bullet point – a small dot or square that is placed before an item or phrase in a list.

Byline – a line at the top of a newspaper or magazine article or report carrying the writer's name.

c–d

Calligram – a poem in which letter formation and font represent aspects of the poem's subject.

Caption – the explanatory wording attached to a picture.

Cast – list of characters (and their actors) in a play.

Causal connective – a linking phrase that confirms cause or effect.

Chapter – a section of writing extending over a number of pages. A change of chapter often heralds the writer's change of focus to a different character or event.

Character – a person (or creature) in a fictional piece of writing.

Chronological order – following the order in which events occur in time.

Cinquain – a poem with a total of 22 syllables in five lines: two, four, six, eight, two syllables.

Cliffhanger – a writing device in which a break occurs in the story when an important character is in danger, or faces a dilemma. The reader is left wondering what will happen.

Clerihew – a short, two-couplet, light-hearted verse about the person named in the first line.

Complex sentence – a sentence that has a main clause and one or more subordinate clauses.

Command sentence – an alternative name for an imperative sentence. It tells the reader what to do.

Concrete poem – a poem that is similar to a shape poem, but is often more subtle and with word repetition. The shape created, often geometrical, adds extra meaning to the poem.

Consonance – the repetition at close intervals of the final consonants of accented syllables in important words.

Contents – a summary of the subject-matter of a book, usually in the form of a list of titles of chapters.

Contraction – shortened form of words that have been combined.

Couplet – two consecutive lines of poetry that function as a pair and usually rhyme.

Culture – the behaviour or beliefs characteristic of a particular social, ethnic or age group.

Custom – usual way of behaving.

Dialect – distinctive grammar and vocabulary of a language, usually linked to geographical area.

Dialogue – speech between two or more characters.

d–h

Dilemma – a problem that presents a choice between two difficult alternatives.

Discussion text – writing that presents all sides of an issue.

Ebook – an electronic book that is a text- and image-based publication in digital form, and is readable on computers or other digital devices.

Editorial – newspaper piece written by or under the responsibility of the editor.

Ellipsis – three dots that show that something has been omitted or is incomplete.

Email – electronic mail that is written and sent to a recipient across the internet or other computer networks.

Fantasy (genre) – imaginary and often highly fanciful ideas in which magic may be included.

Fable – a short story that is written to convey a useful moral lesson. The main characters are usually animals. A moral is written underneath the fable.

Fairy tale – a story written for, or told to, children. It usually includes elements of magic.

Figurative language – expressive language, often using a simile or metaphor, to create a particular impression or mood.

First person – writing from a personal perspective, using *I, we, me* or *us*.

Free verse – a poem that does not have to follow any rhyme or rhythmic rules.

Genre – a grouping of similar texts.

Ghostwriter – a person who may be paid to do most of the writing in someone's autobiography.

Glossary – a part of a text, sometimes included in the appendix, in which the writer defines terms used that are likely to be unfamiliar to the reader.

Haiku – a Japanese poem of 17 syllables in three lines: five, seven, five.

Headline – the title, usually written in large or bold font.

Historical – belonging to the past.

Imagery – the use of language to create a vivid sensory image, often visual.

Imperative verb – the second-person form of the verb that gives a command. The pronoun *you* is not written, merely understood.

Index – an alphabetical list, usually placed at the end of the book, of names and subjects that the writer has mentioned in the book, and the page references.

Interactive material – an electronic resource or game that allows interaction with the user.

Interior monologue – a speech in which a character, alone, thinks aloud.

Issue – important subject or topic.

Italics – faint, sloping writing that distinguishes itself from other text.

Kenning – a list poem, often consisting of expressions about a single subject. Usually, the writer uses just two words for each item and, therefore, each line.

Legend – a traditional story about heroic characters.

List poetry – in a list poem, the writer sometimes repeats a line or phrase.

Literary device – a writing device used to achieve a particular effect, for example, mood or emphasis.

Logical connective – a linking word or phrase that deals with cause and effect.

Media – the means of communication, usually a newspaper, magazine, television, radio or the internet.

Metaphor – writing that describes something as if it were something else. It is a forceful way of comparing two very different things because it says that one thing *is* the other.

Monologue – when one character speaks alone.

Moral (dilemma) – concerned with goodness or badness of character, and the distinction between right and wrong.

Moral (of a story) – the teaching lesson addressed to the reader, written underneath a fable, and advising people how to live.

Myth – an ancient traditional story about gods or heroes.

Narrative poem – a poem that tells a story.

Narrator – a person who remains outside the play's plot and who describes events between the speeches of the other characters.
Non-chronological order – not organised according to the order in which events occur in time.

Online magazine – a magazine that is published electronically, usually on the World Wide Web or internet.
Online newspaper – a newspaper that exists on the World Wide Web or internet, either separately or as an online version of a printed newspaper.
Online resources – word documents and other files available to the reader through the internet.
Onomatopoeia – the use of words that echo sounds associated with their meanings.
Orientation – opening statement sentence(s) that sets the scene for the rest of the recount.

Parable – a short story frequently linked to a religious context, written to illustrate a moral lesson or duty.
Passive – the form of a verb in which the subject of the sentence has the verb's action done to it, for example: *The bacteria are destroyed by high temperatures.* The passive form creates an impersonal style.
Pentameter – a line of poetry with five metrical feet.
Performance poetry – poetry written specifically for oral presentation.
Personification – a form of metaphor, in which language relating to human action is used to refer to non-human things.
Persuasive text – writing that argues a particular point of view.
Phoneme – a unit of sound in a word, represented by one, two, three or four letters.
Phonological – to do with sounds in language.
Planning frame – a page of linked headings, boxes and shapes with spaces for notes and pictures to aid story planning.
Playwright – a dramatist, the person who writes the play.
Plot – the timeline of events in a story.
Production notes – an introduction to a playscript, that may be supplied by the writer to give the reader further information.
Props – accessories used to make a play realistic.

Pun – a play on the meaning of words.

Rap – performance poetry with its roots in the Caribbean and Afro-Caribbean cultures. There is a fast pace, strong rhythm and repetition, and dialect is evident.

Realism – showing life as it is.

Recount – a written retelling of an event or series of events.

Report – a text written to inform a newspaper or magazine reader, often about recent events.

Rhetorical question – a question that does not really need a reply.

Rhyme – the use of words ending in the same sound.

Rhythm – the beat of a poem.

Scene – a portion of a play.

Scenery – the accessories used in theatre to make the stage resemble the supposed place of action.

Science fiction – imaginary, but realistic, speculation about possible events, often in the future.

Sequential connective – a linking phrase that confirms the order of events. It may also be referred to as a 'time connective'.

Setting – the place, time or environment in which events occur.

Shape poetry – poetry in which visual layout (of words, lines and poem) reflects the shape of aspects of the poem's subject.

Simile – a comparison of a subject to something very different, in order to create an image in the reader's mind. It usually uses the word *as* or *like*.

Social – concerned with people's relationships in society.

Sound effects – sounds other than dialogue or music made artificially for use in a play.

Speech mannerism – a speech characteristic such as repetition, sounding pompous, *um* or *er*.

Stage directions – written instructions in the text of the play.

Standfirst – a short sentence that fills out some detail of the story.

Stanza – a set of lines in a poem (a 'verse').

Storyboard – a planning frame, usually pictorial, consisting of sequential boxes to match the story's plot.

Story mountain – a planning frame in the shape of a mountain, with the climax of the story at the top, and events leading to and from the climax forming the sides of the mountain.

Subheading – a further heading placed below the main heading or headline.

Subject line – the place at the head of an email where the writer can type what the email is about.

Subplot – a minor plot that runs in parallel with the main plot.

Syntax – sentence structure: how words are put together in a sentence.

Tanka – a Japanese poem that follows the same syllable pattern as the haiku, but with two additional lines of seven syllables.

Third person – writing from the perspective of another person, using *he*, *she*, *it* or *they*.

Time connective – a linking word associated with time.

Tongue twister – a poem or phrase that relies on alliteration, and hence is difficult to say quickly.

Tradition – belief, opinion or custom passed down from previous generations.

Verse – an alternative word for stanza: a set of lines in a poem.

Website – a collection of linked pages on the World Wide Web (www).

Index

rh-te

th–yo

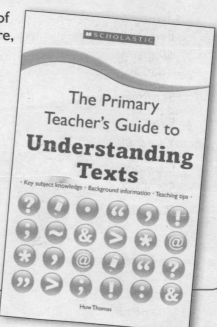

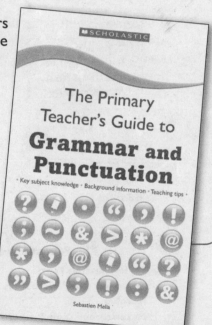

■SCHOLASTIC

Also available in this series:

ISBN 978-1407-12799-6

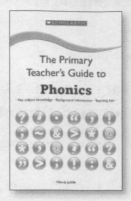

ISBN 978-1407-12796-5

ISBN 978-1407-12797-2

ISBN 978-1407-12809-2

ISBN 978-1407-12795-8

To find out more, call: 0845 603 9091
or visit our website www.scholastic.co.uk